TOPICS **TODAY**

Fake News, Bias, and Media Literacy

By Jennifer Lombardo

Cavendish
Square

New York

Published in 2021 by Cavendish Square Publishing, LLC
243 5th Avenue, Suite 136, New York, NY 10016

First Edition

Website: cavendishsq.com

This publication represents the opinions and views of the author based on his or her personal experience, knowledge, and research. The information in this book serves as a general guide only. The author and publisher have used their best efforts in preparing this book and disclaim liability rising directly or indirectly from the use and application of this book.

Portions of this work were originally authored by Hal Marcovitz and published as *Bias in the Media* (*Hot Topics*). All new material this edition authored by Jennifer Lombardo.

All websites were available and accurate when this book was sent to press.

Library of Congress Cataloging-in-Publication Data

Names: Lombardo, Jennifer, author.
Title: Fake news, bias, and media literacy / Jennifer Lombardo.
Description: First edition. | New York : Cavendish Square Publishing, 2021.
| Series: Topics today | Includes bibliographical references and index.
Identifiers: LCCN 2020003355 (print) | LCCN 2020003356 (ebook) | ISBN 9781502657428 (library binding) | ISBN 9781502657411 (paperback) | ISBN 9781502657435 (ebook)
Subjects: LCSH: Fake news–Juvenile literature. | Media literacy–Juvenile literature.
Classification: LCC PN4784.F27 L66 2021 (print) | LCC PN4784.F27 (ebook)
| DDC 070.4/3–dc23
LC record available at https://lccn.loc.gov/2020003355
LC ebook record available at https://lccn.loc.gov/2020003356

Editor: Jennifer Lombardo
Copy Editor: Michelle Denton
Designer: Deanna Paternostro

Some of the images in this book illustrate individuals who are models. The depictions do not imply actual situations or events.

CPSIA compliance information: Batch #CS20CSQ: For further information contact Cavendish Square Publishing LLC, New York, New York, at 1-877-980-4450.

Printed in China

Find us on

DAILY NEWS

Copyright 1938 by News Syndicate Co., Inc. Reg. U. S. Pat. Off. **NEW YORK'S** PICTURE NEWSPAPER Entered as 2nd class matter, Post Office, New York, N. Y.

FINAL

New York, Monday, October 31, 1938★   48 Pages   2 Cents IN CITY LIMITS | 3 CENTS Elsewhere

KE RADIO 'WAR' TIRS TERROR THROUGH U.S.

—Story on Page 2

(NEWS foto)

Victim

on. WPA ac-
to this radio
St., heard an-
f "smoke in
Running to
broke her arm.

(By Associated Press)

"I Didn't Know". Orson Welles, after broadcast expresses amazement at public reaction. He adapted H. G. Wells' "War of the Worlds" for radio and played principal role. Left: a machine conceived for another H. G. Wells story. Dramatic description of landing of weird "machine from Mars" started last night's panic. —*Story on page 2.*

Average net paid circulation
for September exceeded
Daily---1,800,00
Sunday-3,150,00

Vol. 20. No. 109

FA

S

Introduction

"War"

Caroline Cant
tress, listening
in West 49th
nouncement
Times Square
street, she fell

BECOMING MEDIA SAVVY

A democratic society relies heavily on its free and neutral press. This means that news outlets report the facts of a story as accurately as possible; they don't make up stories or allow anyone—especially the government—to tell them what they're allowed to report. The stories reported by journalists are meant to keep the citizens of a country informed about what's happening around them and keep corruption and crime to a minimum. According to Linda A. Klein, president of the *ABA Journal*, "Lawyers often use information uncovered by journalists to prosecute wrongdoing, to hold officials accountable, and to rectify [correct] injustices."[1] This is why fake news—the knowing publication of untrue stories and the attempt to present them as truth—is such a big problem. Even false accusations of fake news can be disastrous. Once people start losing faith in the media, it becomes much easier for governments to get away with actions that weaken democracy.

Many people already have a low opinion of the media because of the issue of bias. This is when news outlets allow their personal opinions to influence the way they report

In 1938, newspapers reported widespread panic when radio listeners mistook a radio play, *The War of the Worlds*, for a news broadcast about Earth being overrun with aliens. This was fake news; most people weren't fooled by the play, but newspapers exaggerated the incident to try to discredit radio as a news competitor.

issues. Sometimes bias is barely noticeable; other times, it's so strong that it causes journalists to report things incorrectly. All news outlets have bias because reporters are human. Most journalists are aware of the need to avoid bias, but unconscious word choices can influence the way a story is reported. Instead of learning how to spot bias, though, some people choose not to believe anything that's reported in the media.

The internet has further decreased people's trust in the media because it's become increasingly difficult to take things online at face value. One popular meme pokes fun at this phenomenon by attributing the quote "The problem with quotes on the internet is that it is hard to verify their authenticity" to Abraham Lincoln. Sometimes the meme is accompanied by a picture of Benjamin Franklin, implying that he is Lincoln. This meme points out that just because something can be found online doesn't mean it's true.

People often use false statements and misleading photos to influence others' opinions, and if they do their job well enough, they can sometimes even affect things such as the way people cast their votes for certain candidates or policies. Thinking critically about information in the media—also known as media literacy—is more important than ever in an age where anyone with an internet connection can present their opinions as fact without providing any kind of proof.

What Does Bias Look Like?

Bias can emerge in several ways. One reason for biased reporting is to attract viewers who hold a certain viewpoint. For instance, Fox News tends to attract conservative viewers, while CNN tends to attract liberal viewers. Other news outlets and blogs are generally also slanted in one direction or another—some much more than others. Another reason for bias is that journalists and media company owners sometimes want to use their power to promote political leaders and the policies they favor. Sometimes bias can be very subtle. A journalist may develop a preconceived notion of how a story should be told before they conduct the first interviews. In such cases, the reporter will often seek out interviewees who can be counted on to provide comments that will be in agreement with the way the journalist sees the story.

Media bias is not a new problem. In 2001, a series of race riots erupted in Cincinnati, Ohio, after a white police officer shot an unarmed black man. White readers of the *Cincinnati Enquirer* newspaper were truly shocked when they read the stories about the rioting; they couldn't figure out why black people were so angry about this one incident. What they didn't know was that black community leaders had been making reports about the police for months, stating that black citizens had been abused and harassed by white police officers.

White readers of the *Enquirer* weren't aware of the police abuses or the simmering anger in the black community because the newspaper had ignored the issue. Because the *Enquirer* hadn't assigned reporters to cover the issue more fully and because the mostly white members of the news staff had few sources in the black community, the newspaper's executives and journalists, like everyone else in Cincinnati, were unprepared when the racial unrest erupted into violence. The *Enquirer* committed bias by neglect: By ignoring the problems in the black community, the newspaper's coverage gave the false impression to its readers that race relations in Cincinnati were healthy and progressive.

Following the riots in Cincinnati, the *Enquirer* took steps to increase understanding of problems in the black community. Along with other community service and education groups, the newspaper helped organize a series of town hall meetings in which members of the community, sociologists, members of the newspaper staff, city political leaders, and others were encouraged to discuss race relations. About 2,100 people participated in 145 community meetings sponsored by the newspaper. Following the meetings, the *Enquirer* used its editorial pages to urge the city to rehabilitate impoverished neighborhoods rather than commit its resources to upscale shopping districts. *Enquirer* editorials also urged Cincinnati school administrators to add courses on racial tolerance to the curricula of city schools. The newspaper even provided resources to Cincinnati teachers to help them talk about racism in their

Because the *Cincinnati Enquirer* had ignored the issues that were affecting the black community, white residents were shocked when a riot erupted in response to the police shooting of an unarmed black teen. Shown here is a photograph from the riot.

classes, creating a database on its website of stories and reports about racial issues.

The paper did many things to correct its mistake, but unfortunately, this rarely happens in other instances of media bias. This means it's often up to the reader or viewer to learn media literacy skills, such as the ability to identify different types of media and understand what kind of message they're trying to send. Paying attention to things such as who's funding a media outlet, what words people use in videos and articles, and what kind of view is being promoted are all parts of media literacy. Using these skills, viewers and readers can do their own research into what's being presented to them to determine what's real and what's fake news.

CHAPTER ONE

UNDERSTANDING BIAS AND FAKE NEWS

Many people have only a partial understanding of what constitutes media bias and fake news. Some people think that if coverage of a particular story changes over time, the reporter was lying or mistaken at one point. However, it's important to remember that news changes every day. This sounds obvious, but it's something people often fail to take into account when they evaluate changing news coverage. News outlets report on stories as they happen. This means the story changes as new facts are uncovered. For instance, during and after a natural disaster or mass shooting, the number of casualties is continuously reported to the news as rescue workers find out more. Sometimes people die a day or two after the initial incident because they were badly injured. If a news outlet reports 10 casualties one day and 15 the next, it's not because they're inflating the number to sound worse; they just have more information. This happens all the time. Things that were once thought to be true might later be proven false, and vice versa. Sometimes people say things to reporters that are later found to be deliberate lies; other times, journalists will dig into a person's statements and find out that, although the person thought they were telling the truth, they were mistaken. Changing news coverage is not the same thing as bias or fake news.

◀ For decades, public faith in the media has been declining around the world.

Although media bias has been around as long as there have been news outlets, the term "fake news" has increasingly been used since the 2016 US presidential election. This generally refers to stories that are outright lies. However, the term is not always used accurately. Some stories that are labeled fake news are indeed completely made up, but the label is increasingly used to discredit any story with which a person disagrees. Both fake news and the misuse of the term to describe real news stories can have dangerous consequences.

Understanding media bias is important, but knowing media bias exists can also have a dangerous effect. In some cases, people will invent stories and try to give them credibility by claiming that the media is too biased to report them. This can further complicate things; people are aware that the mainstream media does ignore certain stories, but it can be difficult—sometimes impossible—to figure out which stories are truly being ignored and which are being promoted by people who want to sway the opinions of others.

Following a Code of Ethics

Although media bias exists, journalism is a profession that operates under a code of standards and ethics designed largely to ensure that bias doesn't affect the news too much. Many news organizations try to follow certain standards of good journalism that have evolved over the course of more than two centuries. This code of ethics isn't law, and there's no punishment for not following it. A news source that is reputable, or trustworthy, will follow this code simply because the reporters believe it's the right thing to do.

In most cases, individual news outlets have developed their own rules and ethical standards so their reporters and editors know what is expected of them as they report the news. The *New York Times*, for example, has a guide that's issued to its reporters and editors which specifies that they have a responsibility to remain impartial observers at news events, that they aren't permitted to receive money or gifts from the people or organizations they cover, and that they must not enter into romantic relationships with the people they cover. In addition, sportswriters are prohibited from gambling on sporting events, movie critics may not invest in films that are in production,

Liberal or Conservative?

Journalists are often accused of having either a liberal or conservative bias. These two ideologies, or belief systems, form the basis for most mainstream political thought in America today. Each ideology traces its roots back hundreds of years to the emergence of democracy in Europe, when liberals advocated swift and decisive change while conservatives preached caution and gradual change.

Liberalism and conservatism have changed over time and now mean slightly different things in modern American society. According to Geoffrey R. Stone, a law professor at the University of Chicago, liberals, or those on the "left" of the political spectrum, question authority but generally remain respectful of different opinions and ways of life. He says liberals look to the government to protect individual liberties and help those who need it. Stone wrote, "It is liberals who maintain that a national community is like a family and that government exists in part to 'promote the general welfare.'"[1]

Modern conservatives, or those on the "right," also stand for individual freedoms, but they maintain that government should play a limited role in society. Conservative editor Erick Erickson summed up the general values of most conservatives this way: "Government that does the least is best. The individual is of greater value to society than the collective mob. As an individual succeeds, the nation as a whole succeeds ... Power in the hands of a few is bad and collectivism is a disaster ... Free markets coupled with free people will benefit us all better than a government picking winners and losers."[2]

1. Geoffrey R. Stone, "Liberal Values," *HuffPost*, modified May 25, 2011, www.huffingtonpost.com/geoffrey-r-stone/liberal-values_b_31218.html.

2. Erick Erickson, "What Does It Mean to Be Conservative?," RealClear Politics, 2018, www.realclearpolitics.com/articles/2018/08/03/what_does_it_mean_to_be_conservative_137701.html.

and travel writers may not accept free trips from tour promoters. These rules are designed to ensure that the newspaper or website remains trustworthy and neutral. For instance, if a sportswriter loses a bet on a team they're covering, the sportswriter may take out their grudge on the team in print; similarly, if a movie critic has invested in a film, that critic's review of the film will undoubtedly be positive, regardless of how good or bad the film may be. The paper's policy on ethics in journalism states:

> The goal of The New York Times is to cover the news as impartially as possible … and to treat readers, news sources, advertisers and others fairly and openly, and to be seen to be doing so. The reputation of The Times rests upon such perceptions, and so do the professional reputations of its staff members. Thus The Times and members of its news department and editorial page staff share an interest in avoiding conflicts of interest or an appearance of a conflict.[1]

Journalists often conduct interviews to let people share their side of a story, but they aren't supposed to tell people what to say.

The ethical standards under which most news organizations operate are similar. In their book, *The Elements of Journalism*, Bill Kovach and Tom Rosenstiel identified several practices that are necessary for good journalism. The American Press Institute created a list of the most important:

- The first obligation of the journalist is to tell the truth.
- A journalist's first loyalty is to citizens, not a government or company
- All information presented in a news story must be verifiable as fact.
- Journalists must maintain independence from those they cover.
- Journalism must monitor those in power without being influenced by them.
- Journalism must provide a way for citizens to voice criticism.
- Journalism must provide information that is relevant to people's lives and do so in a way that is interesting to read.
- Journalists must keep the news in proper perspective, not inflating the importance of minor issues or minimizing the significance of major developments.
- Journalists must possess a conscience and moral compass.

In a perfect world, journalists and editors as well as the people who own newspapers, TV networks, radio stations, and websites would adhere to these principles. According to the American Press Institute, even regular citizens have a duty to follow these rules when they report on social media about things that are happening around them. However, violations of these principles occur regularly.

Many news professionals have spent their entire careers following the principles of ethical journalism, but some have not. The history of the American media is filled with stories of journalists as well as wealthy press barons dictating how their newspapers and broadcast networks should cover and slant the news.

Bias is not always political; sometimes it can be used to hurt a person or institution financially. For example, Walter Annenberg built up a media empire that included his hometown newspapers,

A Different Point of View

Although news outlets have a duty to publish facts, they also frequently publish opinions separately from news stories. These opinion pieces are important because they give people different perspectives based on the facts of a matter, allowing them to consider angles they may never have thought of before. News outlets publish opinions in a number of ways. For example, most newspapers publish editorials. Typically, the page that features editorials is set aside specifically for that purpose and will be clearly marked to advise readers that they aren't reading news stories. Editorials represent the position of the newspaper on issues of public importance. They're generally written by members of the newspaper staff who don't cover stories or otherwise participate in the news-gathering function of the paper. They don't include bylines, which identify the authors. A newspaper's editorial positions are crafted by members of the paper's editorial board, who meet to discuss the issues and decide how the paper's editorial page should respond. Editorial boards often include senior editors, editorial page staff members, and representatives from the papers' corporate offices. Members of the community may be invited to join editorial boards.

the *Philadelphia Inquirer* and *Philadelphia Daily News*, as well as *TV Guide* and *Seventeen* magazines and local radio and TV stations. For years, Annenberg wouldn't allow the names of certain celebrities to be published if he didn't like them because he didn't want to give them publicity. In addition to celebrities, Annenberg also harbored a bias against the Philadelphia Warriors, a professional basketball team, most likely because the Warriors engaged in a rental dispute with Annenberg, who owned the arena where they played their games. In retaliation, Annenberg banned news of the Warriors from his newspapers, refusing to send a sportswriter to cover their games. Soon, this lack of publicity for the team hurt the Warriors financially, forcing the team to leave Philadelphia. "There were no game stories, no features, no line scores, no mention in the NBA standings box

Op-eds were originally published on the page opposite the editorial page, which is how they got their name. Op-eds are bylined, meaning the author is identified. Op-eds express the opinions of the writers, who don't work for the newspaper and are often recognized as experts in specific fields, such as politics and law. Columns, which are also bylined, are generally written by members of the newspaper staff who are specifically assigned to comment on issues in the news.

Newspapers also publish letters to the editor, expressing the opinions of readers. Most newspapers' websites also invite readers to add their comments at the ends of the articles or through blogs maintained to air public discussion on specific issues.

The simple fact that news outlets are publishing opinions doesn't make them biased; rather, they're providing readers and viewers with ideas based on logic. Mike Argento, a columnist for the *York Daily Record* in Pennsylvania and former president of the National Society of Newspaper Columnists, explained, "Our job isn't to report rumors or to throw out opinions that are not based on fact or to report opinions as fact."[1]

1. Mike Argento, "Prez Column," National Society of Newspaper Columnists, October 26, 2008, www.columnists.com/2008/10/prez-column.

and promotional ads were rejected," wrote Annenberg's biographer, Christopher Ogden. "Game attendance plummeted."[2]

Although Annenberg's low regard for certain celebrities was likely centered on personal biases, his bias against the Warriors seemed to stem from his financial dispute with the team. As such, he was willing to resort to using the power of the media he controlled to hurt the team financially and drive it out of the city.

Bias in Reporting

Bias is not only shown by the powerful people who run news outlets. Many studies of American media have uncovered bias at the reporting level, where journalists report their stories in ways that show their own beliefs and preconceived notions of what the story should say even before they have all the facts. This occurs even though college journalism students are taught from the first day of their first reporting class to be unbiased, fair, and accurate in their reporting.

A 2005 study by former University of California, Los Angeles (UCLA) political scientist Tim Groseclose and University of Missouri economist Jeffrey Milyo examined the issue of bias in the American media. Groseclose and Milyo used a number of factors in comparing the work of several well-known news organizations, such as the sources they cited and the types of stories they covered. They didn't assess editorials, opinion columns, letters to the editor, or other places where opinions are given—only the content of the publications or on-air time devoted to "straight news" stories. The authors concluded that many of the most popular news outlets in America, including the *New York Times*, *Washington Post*, and *USA Today*, showed a strong liberal bias. However, other studies have found the opposite result. In 2012, a similar study by Daniel Quackenbush at Elon University found a strong conservative bias in many major media outlets.

Unfortunately, studies about media bias have some degree of unreliability. Dave D'Alessio, associate professor of communication at the University of Connecticut, has studied media bias for years. He explained the problem with trying to assess media bias in most cases:

> Broadly speaking, I don't trust anybody that says the media are biased because the very nature of bias is that it's a perception— it's something that people see and they base it on what they see. There's something called a hostile media effect. Basically whenever people are engaged in an issue ... they see coverage as biased against their perception, no matter what it is.[3]

This doesn't mean media bias doesn't exist; it simply means that people who are claiming the media is biased against their view may be ignoring certain facts. For instance, President Donald Trump has claimed frequently that certain media outlets are biased against him and has been quick to declare that negative news articles are "fake news," even when the facts in a story can be proven beyond a doubt. Many of his supporters take this view as well, while in the eyes of many of his opponents, the opposite is true: They tend not to believe anything good about him, even things that can be proven to be true.

Some people also believe journalists and news outlets choose not to cover certain stories that don't align with their biases. However, a study published in *Science Advances* in 2020 found this to be false. The researchers stated that "*despite being dominantly liberals/*

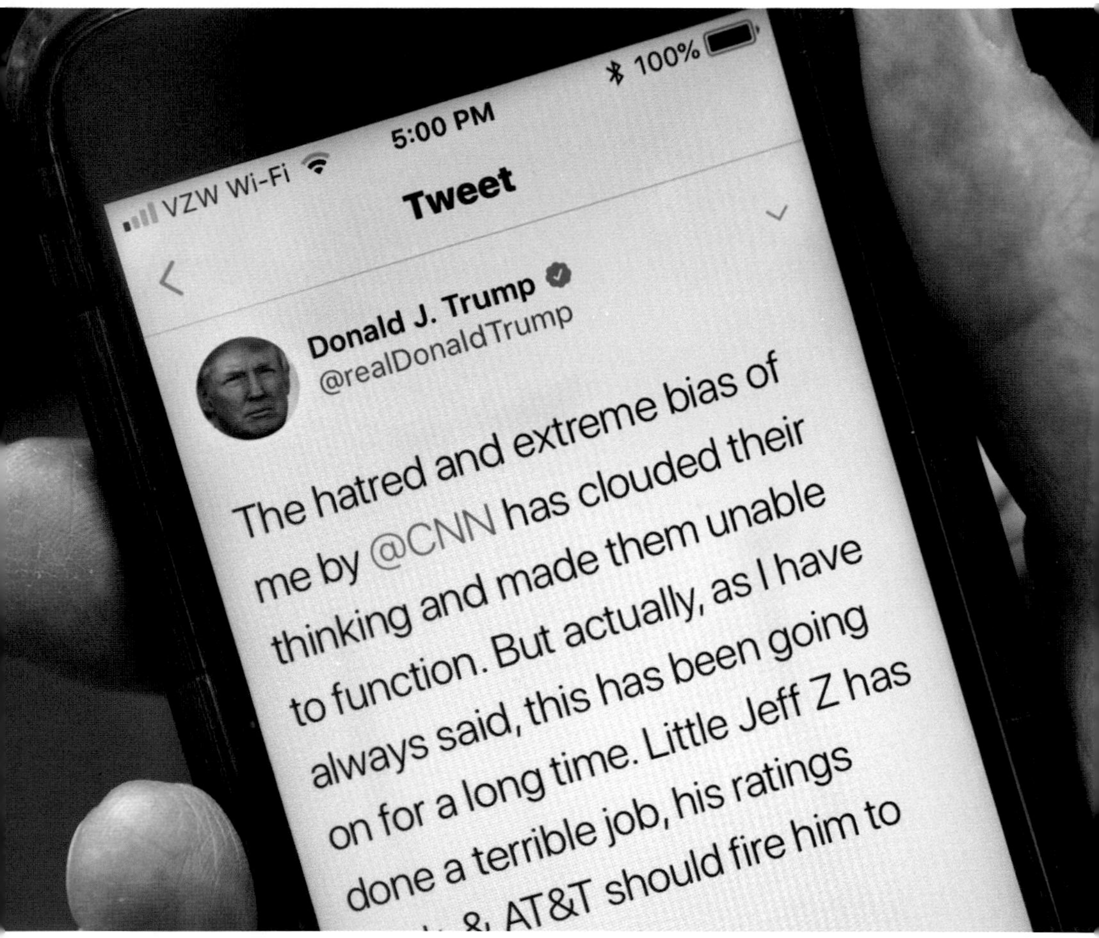

VZW Wi-Fi
5:00 PM
100%
Tweet
Donald J. Trump
@realDonaldTrump
The hatred and extreme bias of me by @CNN has clouded their thinking and made them unable to function. But actually, as I have always said, this has been going on for a long time. Little Jeff Z has done a terrible job, his ratings
AT&T should fire him to

Since he took office in 2016, President Trump has claimed that many news outlets are biased against him. Shown here is a tweet from 2018 referencing Jeff Zucker, the president of CNN.

Democrats, journalists do not seem to be exhibiting liberal media bias (or conservative media bias) in what they choose to cover … showing that overall, journalists do not display political gatekeeping bias in the stories they choose to cover."[4]

Many reporters do a very good job of being fair and unbiased, but sometimes the bias comes across in subtle ways that the reporter doesn't realize have added a slant to the story. Groseclose and Milyo cited one story, published in the *Washington Times*—a conservative news organization, not to be confused with the more liberal *Washington Post*—reporting an act of Congress that provided $300,000 to restore opera houses in Connecticut, Michigan, and Washington. The average conservative who opposes unnecessary government spending might be angry and consider this a wasteful use of taxpayer money. The story is technically accurate, but Groseclose and Milyo pointed out that the reporter could have provided a fairer and generally unbiased story about the opera house grants if they had also included the fact that $300,000 is a tiny fraction of a federal budget that spends more than $3 trillion a year. Other reporters may seek out sources that are guaranteed to give inflammatory quotes. If these are the only quotes in the story, they can severely slant the way the story is presented.

Even though it faces accusations of bias, there's no question that the press continues to serve an important role in American society. Reporters have enabled people to witness events in other countries up close. They have provided information on crucial events—including assassinations of presidents, the terrorist attacks of September 11, 2001, and the devastation of hurricanes and other disasters—to readers and viewers anxious for details. Reporters keep people up to date on important events that affect their lives, such as presidential scandals, potentially dangerous situations, and economic trends. As journalist Kara Hackett wrote, "The real question is not a matter of whether our news is biased or not. It's more about the degree to which reporters make an effort to present an educated, well-researched account of what's going on. And as we know from our history books, while the facts are indisputable, they can look differently to different people."[5] When journalists do their job right, the media can influence society and act as a catalyst for social change. However, when reporters and news executives permit their biases to affect the way they do their jobs, they can harm the credibility of all media outlets and have a negative impact on the government and society as a whole.

Exciting but Not Informative

An important way in which bias emerges is the style in which news outlets choose to report on events. In an era where ratings and advertising are important considerations for the news media, an engaging story is essential. The news isn't just a means of spreading information; it's also a source of income for its operators.

This bias has become very apparent in recent presidential primaries and elections. If voters are to make a decision about who to elect, they need to be well informed of a candidate's policies, experience, and leadership qualities. However, a report from the Harvard Kennedy School's Shorenstein Center on Media, Politics and Public Policy found that during the 2016 primary elections, only 11 percent of media coverage focused on the candidates' actual qualifications.

Instead of essential information, reporting focused heavily on the "horse race"—stories about which candidates were winning and losing. These reports were devoted to poll results, delegates won, amounts of money raised, and strategies used by the candidates during the primary process. The results of early elections strongly influenced how the news depicted a candidate, as "leading" or "losing," and would focus on their ability to win small contests rather than their ability to be president. This often led to more positive coverage for any candidate with a lead in votes and negative coverage for candidates trailing behind. When it comes time for a voter to decide, they often only have access to information about how a candidate has been succeeding or failing in the election process, rather than a useful discussion of their abilities. It's not until after the primary process is over that a meaningful conversation on the candidates' qualities enters the news—after the votes have been cast and it's too late for voters to change their minds.

This same discussion of the media coverage of presidential primaries was in the spotlight again in 2020, when many people called out the media's focus on certain candidates seen as "winning" after early primary victories and poll results and their ignoring of other candidates and their policies.

While many agree that there should be better reporting of an event with such far-reaching consequences, the nature of the

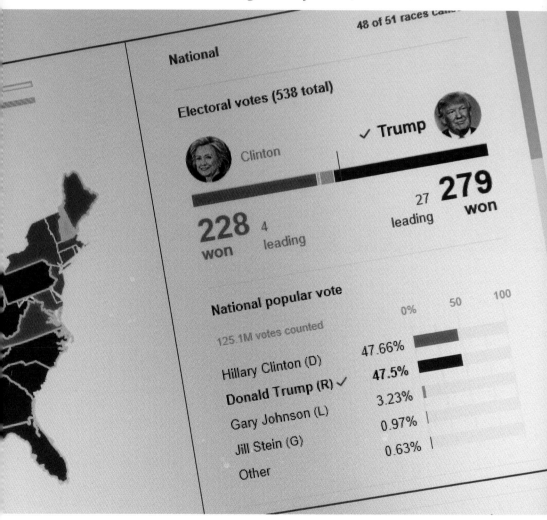

National

Electoral votes (538 total)

✓ **Trump**

Clinton

228 4
won   leading

27 **279**
leading   won

National popular vote

0%   50   100

125.1M votes counted

Hillary Clinton (D)   47.66%

Donald Trump (R) ✓   47.5%

Gary Johnson (L)   3.23%

Jill Stein (G)   0.97%

Other   0.63%

During a presidential campaign, the media tends to report more on who's winning or losing than on each candidate's policies. Shown here are the results of the 2016 presidential race.

presidential campaign makes it difficult to avoid the horse race style of reporting. The election process is long and involves the entire country. Journalists feel obligated to report on things that feel fresh and interesting. A candidate's policy and background don't change on a day-to-day basis, but the actions they take during the campaign do. When a candidate's policies are reported during a campaign, journalists generally discuss how those policies could help or hurt the candidate in a particular contest. Detailed conversations about the issues are much more rare.

Your Opinion Matters!

1. Why do you think many journalists are liberals, as shown in certain studies?

2. How can columnists, editorial writers, and commentators avoid accusations of bias?

3. Give an example of media bias you've seen recently.

CHAPTER TWO

COMBINING NEWS AND ENTERTAINMENT

Many people perceive the news as boring. When people are bored by the news, they don't watch or read it, which spells trouble for a news outlet's profits. In an effort to gain viewers, news outlets on cable channels have started changing the way news is reported. When one network gains viewers with these changes, others tend to do the same to remain competitive. Over time, this creates a change in the way most news is reported and influences which stories are given the spotlight.

Rather than simply reading the day's events, cable networks now tend to present news in the most dramatic and polarizing manner possible. Polarizing means offering two extreme opinions with very little middle ground and encouraging people to take one position or the other. This makes it difficult for people to work together to solve problems in their country, but it also creates drama that's good for network ratings. The mission to inform has become a mission to entertain.

With this change in the way news is presented, viewership for cable news networks has dramatically increased over the years. With an average of 2.5 million viewers every

◀ In the past, when the news placed less emphasis on entertainment, it was generally seen as more trustworthy. Walter Cronkite, a CBS news anchor throughout the 1960s and 1970s, was named "the most trusted man in America" in a 1972 opinion poll.

night, Fox News is the most-watched cable channel in America. The second most-watched cable channel, MSNBC, averages 1.5 million viewers per night. These two channels are the only news networks in the top 10 most-watched cable channels; the other eight are entertainment channels, including HGTV, TLC, the Hallmark Channel, and ESPN.

The Evolution of Cable News

At first, the presentation of news on cable TV resembled the typical news formats found on most local and network broadcasts: Essentially, a news anchor sat behind a desk, reading a straightforward account of the news while airing stories by reporters in the field. This is the format viewers saw in 1980 when the Cable News Network (CNN), the first cable channel to devote itself entirely to news, aired its first broadcast.

CNN was founded by Ted Turner, a businessman from Atlanta, Georgia, who made his fortune selling advertising space on billboards. Turner was among the first entrepreneurs to realize the potential of cable television. He invested heavily in the cable business, buying TV stations and marketing their programming over the nation's growing cable TV systems. In 1980, he launched CNN, featuring news programming 24 hours a day, 7 days a week. Eventually, Turner sold CNN to Time Warner.

CNN had the cable news universe virtually to itself until 1996, when two competitors debuted: MSNBC and Fox News Channel. MSNBC was established by the NBC network in a joint venture with Microsoft. At first, given Microsoft's influence, the network's interests were supposed to focus on technological and scientific developments that would be of interest to consumers, such as trends in computer and cell phone technology. However, that format was soon dropped in favor of straight news coverage, talk shows, and politically oriented interview shows.

Meanwhile, Fox News was launched by Australian-born news baron Rupert Murdoch, who also owned the conservative newspapers the *Wall Street Journal* and the *New York Post* as well as several other media properties. Murdoch's first move was to put

Fox News is the most-watched cable network in the United States—and one of the most controversial. Shown here are signs encouraging people to boycott, or avoid, Fox News's sponsors so the channel will have less money.

Roger Ailes in charge of Fox News. Ailes had been associated with conservative causes for many years and served as a media adviser to Republican presidents Richard Nixon, Ronald Reagan, and George H. W. Bush. With Ailes in charge of Fox News, the network soon developed an undeniably conservative slant. Despite the arrival of MSNBC and Fox News, CNN was still the ratings leader among the cable news networks. This was due mostly to the widespread popularity of interviewers such as Larry King, who was the host of a nightly talk show.

In the fall of 2000, as the country was riveted by the unfolding drama of the disputed presidential election of

Concerns About Fox News

Fox News has always had a conservative bias, meaning it tends to criticize politicians on the left and applaud those on the right. However, even when a news outlet has a political leaning, it's supposed to remain apart from the affairs it reports on. A journalist's job is to report the news, not to influence it. They should also report the facts of an issue even when they go against the journalist's personal political views. All of these are basic parts of the journalistic code of ethics, but since Donald Trump took office in 2016, media scholars as well as the general public have started to voice concerns about the direction Fox has taken.

Trump has made no secret of the fact that Fox is his favorite news network. Vox explained why this has become a problem:

People are increasingly questioning whether [Fox] has crossed a line in the Trump era and become an outright propaganda operation ... There's plenty of evidence to support the argument. Trump constantly watches Fox News, tweets out claims he hears on the network, reportedly speaks regularly with Sean Hannity [a host on the network], and gives the majority of his interviews to Fox News. World leaders as well as members of Congress quickly learned that one of the best ways to communicate a message to Trump is to say it on Fox News.[1]

George W. Bush, Bill O'Reilly, who at the time hosted *The O'Reilly Factor* on Fox News, surged past King in the ratings. O'Reilly pioneered a much different type of cable host than King. Instead of being friendly and conversational like King, O'Reilly was confrontational, opinionated, and conservative in his outlook. His aggressive style soon attracted a large and dedicated audience, mainly made up of conservatives. By 2009, O'Reilly was hosting the top-rated show on cable news. Until he was dismissed from the network in 2017, his show maintained high ratings.

O'Reilly routinely confronted guests with tough questions and, if he disagreed with them, wasn't above referring to them

Media scholar Tom Rosenstiel agreed that certain segments aired on Fox News now count as government propaganda. He explained that this is because Trump and certain members of the network, such as the anchors on *Fox & Friends*, knowingly work together. Trump is watching the show, "and they know it, and know that he is in turn tweeting out things they say while the show is still on and that those tweets are being picked up. This is an active collaboration, and it's conscious and direct … The same thing is true, but even more so, of Trump and Sean Hannity. Hannity and the president reportedly talk almost every day. Hannity advises Trump on messaging. Hannity then echoes much of that messaging on his program."[2]

This kind of active cooperation between a news network and the president is often seen as dangerous for the public. People who watch Fox News, especially the segments Rosenstiel mentioned, are generally getting only information that's been directly approved by the president. Furthermore, Trump has attempted to discredit competing news outlets—especially those that report negative things about him, even when those things are true—as "fake news." This creates a scenario in which people believe the only network that's telling them the truth is the one that's working directly with the government.

1. Sean Illing, "How Fox News Evolved into a Propaganda Operation," Vox, March 22, 2019, www.vox.com/2019/3/22/18275835/fox-news-trump-propaganda-tom-rosenstiel.

2. Quoted in Illing, "How Fox News Evolved."

in derogatory terms—for instance, one of his favorite insults was "pinhead." In 2007, journalism professors at Indiana University conducted an analysis of *The O'Reilly Factor* and concluded that in the show's opening segment, in which O'Reilly delivered a commentary, the host used a derogatory term for a person or group every 6.8 seconds. According to Mike Conway, one of the study's authors, "It's obvious he's very big into calling people names, and he's very big into glittering generalities … He's not very subtle. He's going to call people names, or he's going to paint

Choosing Comfort

Although there is certainly bias in the media, individuals play a role in the spread and persistence of misinformation. Psychologists call this information avoidance: the tendency of humans to believe what they want to believe because it makes them happier or more comfortable. Sometimes this means ignoring certain information, while other times it means seeking out the information that makes people happiest—for instance, by only watching a news channel that aligns with a person's views. Carnegie Mellon University explained why this is a problem:

Questionable evidence is often treated as credible when it confirms what someone wants to believe—as is the case of discredited research linking vaccines to autism. And evidence that meets the rigorous demands of science is often discounted if it goes against what people want to believe, as illustrated by widespread dismissal of climate change.

Information avoidance can be harmful, for example, when people miss opportunities to treat serious diseases early on or fail to learn about better financial investments that could prepare them for retirement. It also has large societal implications.[1]

The researchers explained that giving people information that contradicts their beliefs doesn't work because people something in a positive [or negative] way, often without any real evidence to support that viewpoint."[1]

O'Reilly also regularly sent producers out in the field to stage what are known as ambush interviews. Typically, the producer and a camera crew confront someone on the street—generally an unsuspecting politician, celebrity, or other newsmaker—shouting questions and demanding answers while waving a microphone in the interview subject's face. In 2009, the *New York Times* estimated that O'Reilly's producers had conducted about 50 ambush

will often simply ignore it. In some cases, being proven wrong will actually strengthen a person's belief that they're correct, especially if the information is presented aggressively. They suggested that it's better for people to "find ways not only to expose people to conflicting information, but to increase people's receptivity to information that challenges what they believe and want to believe."[2]

The popular truTV series *Adam Ruins Everything* discussed this in August 2017. The series, which is intended to show people that things they believe may actually be wrong, aired a segment about what it called "the backfire effect": "One study found that when people concerned about side effects of the flu shot were informed it was safe, they actually became less willing to get it ... Because when you try to change someone's mind, the other person often feels attacked."[3]

This is why people who hold a particular belief that's reinforced by the news they read or watch will often discount contradictory information and see it as evidence of bias, even when it's not. A large part of this is an unwillingness to feel unintelligent or easily tricked.

1. Shilo Rea, "Information Avoidance: How People Select Their Own Reality," Carnegie Mellon University, March 13, 2017, www.cmu.edu/news/stories/archives/2017/march/information-avoidance.html.

2. Quoted in Rea, "Information Avoidance."

3. truTV, "Adam Ruins Everything—Why Proving Someone Wrong Often Backfires," YouTube video, 1:39, August 24, 2017, www.youtube.com/watch?v=Q8NydsXl32s.

interviews over the course of the previous 3 years, and the targets, for the most part, were liberal political leaders or others who had been critical of Republicans. "When the subjects don't answer," wrote *New York Times* media critic Brian Stelter, "the questions become more provocative and emotional."[2] Ambush interviews are considered by many journalists to be in poor taste, but many viewers find them appealing because the results tend to be more dramatic than planned interviews.

Fox also added other conservative commentators to its line-up, and they have carved out their own styles of interviewing guests and providing opinions on the news. Among them is Sean Hannity, who marked President Barack Obama's 100th day in office by playing a video showing various political leaders fighting among themselves and Obama administration officials admitting to mistakes while ominous music played in the background—all meant to illustrate that the liberal Obama administration had gotten off to a rocky start.

As Fox News Channel's audience expanded, MSNBC was blazing its own path. After dropping its emphasis on technological news, the network started putting together a lineup of liberal commentators that included hosts Keith Olbermann and Rachel Maddow. Each host has added their own dramatic touches to their commentaries. For example, during the George W. Bush administration, Olbermann featured a nightly spot on his show, *Countdown*, that he named "Bushed." The feature was devoted, he said, to the 50 running scandals of the Bush administration, and in each spot, Olbermann highlighted a different example of what he claimed to be wrongdoings by members of the Republican's administration.

MSNBC's audience hasn't grown quite as large as that of Fox. However, as each network's audience has grown, it hasn't been at the expense of the other's. It's clear that both networks are aiming for niche audiences—"true believers" who aren't looking for objective reporting but for commentators to present versions of the news that will strike a chord with their own personal biases. Indeed, Fox News commentators readily admit that their audience is drawn from people who are frustrated with the mainstream media, which they have accused of harboring a liberal bias. According to Diana Mutz, professor of political science and communications at the University of Pennsylvania, "It's nothing new for people to seek media with their values ... Cable now offers people more choices; it can narrowcast to smaller, yet still profitable audiences."[3]

Misleading Viewers

As cable commentators withhold facts or embellish the truth, their viewers sit at home absorbing those messages. Studies have started to show that many viewers have been unable to cut through the noise of what they hear and see on TV and the internet and have developed some serious misperceptions about world events.

Many cable news networks have a strong focus on entertainment, and sometimes this causes them to sacrifice

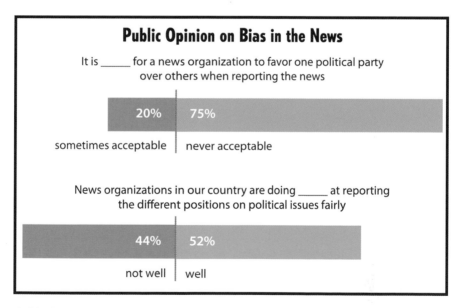

Public Opinion on Bias in the News

It is _____ for a news organization to favor one political party over others when reporting the news

| 20% | 75% |

sometimes acceptable | never acceptable

News organizations in our country are doing _____ at reporting the different positions on political issues fairly

| 44% | 52% |

not well | well

A 2016 survey of 38 countries by the Pew Research Center found that most people prefer unbiased news. However, as shown here, 44 percent of people polled said they didn't think their news organizations were doing well at giving unbiased reports.

factual information. The independent website Media Bias/Fact Check gave MSNBC and CNN a rating of "mostly factual" because hosts frequently report accurate information but occasionally make false statements. Fox News has received a rating of "mixed" for its factual accuracy. In fact, a 2012 study by Fairleigh Dickinson University found that people who watch Fox News tend to be less informed about the reality of current events than people who watch other news networks. This has become known as the "Fox News effect." However, *Forbes* magazine published an article by William Poundstone, author of *Head in the Cloud: Why Knowing Things Still Matters When Facts Are So Easy to Look Up,* in which Poundstone pointed out that correlation does not equal causation. This means watching Fox News may not cause people to be less informed; instead, it's more likely that people who are already uninformed choose to watch Fox News more than any other network. However, Fox News doesn't help its viewers be any better informed. Poundstone noted, "There are important stories that don't make anyone angry, prove liberals are evil or otherwise carry an emotional punch. Fox viewers get less of them."[4] Some people say Fox News is more accurately called an entertainment channel than a news channel.

In a less scientific study, staffers of *Jimmy Kimmel Live!* went out onto the street in 2013 to ask people whether they preferred Obamacare or the Affordable Care Act (ACA). These are two names for the same health care program; however, many conservative news outlets dislike the ACA and call it Obamacare as a derogatory term. It's been called Obamacare so often that the name has stuck, and most people are unaware its true name is the ACA—something that was proven when people answered Jimmy Kimmel's question by saying that they were strongly against one program and believed the other was much better. The answers they gave depended on their political views: People who supported Obama tended to say Obamacare was better than the ACA, and the reverse was true for people who disliked Obama.

Shows such as *Jimmy Kimmel Live!* often mix the news with jokes. They aren't reputable news sources and don't claim to be.

Throughout the 2016 presidential election process, the ACA was a major part of candidates' platforms, so it was featured in the news often. Some news outlets called it Obamacare, while others called it the ACA. Reporters sometimes made it clear that these were the same program, but often they didn't. In 2017, *Jimmy Kimmel Live!* repeated the experiment to see if the heavy news coverage of the issue had made people aware that the programs were one and the same. However, they found many people who still believed they were different. This not only shows that the media often doesn't give all the facts about an issue, but also that people tend to have difficulty sorting out the information they hear from different sources. However, it's important to remember that *Jimmy Kimmel Live!* is an entertainment program, not a news program, so it only aired interviews with people who were unaware of the difference, as this is generally funnier to audiences; most likely there were many people who knew the correct answer to the question.

When people hear different statements from different sources, they tend to assume that one of those statements is actually a lie—and often they pick the statement they most agree with rather than the one that has the most evidence to back it up. Many cable news viewers pay close attention to what they see and hear on the channels they watch, and what they see and hear quite often falls short of the truth. Frequently, when they do eventually hear the truth, they will assume it was made up to promote a particular agenda and dismiss it as "fake news" rather than doing their own research and getting all the facts.

Biased on Purpose

As people have shown an increasing preference for biased news, it's unsurprising that extremely biased entertainment shows have grown incredibly. *The Daily Show with Jon Stewart* pioneered this trend. Jon Stewart became the host of *The Daily Show* in 1999 and, over the course of his 16-year run, helped turn it into one of the most popular shows on TV. He mainly targeted politicians but also found that he could get a lot of laughs by making fun of cable TV journalists. Each night, Stewart would run clips of cable news reporters overdramatizing the news, showing their obvious biases and fumbling with the high-tech graphics that illustrated the news. In 2015, Stewart stepped down as host and Trevor Noah kept the show going.

Media critics have suggested that Stewart earned the trust of viewers because—unlike many cable news commentators—he didn't try to represent opinions and drama as news, but told his viewers right up front that what they were about to see was all in fun. However, it's undeniably true that Stewart had his own frequently liberal biases and sometimes used his show to condemn the actions of politicians, giving his own opinion of the news pieces he featured. As *The Daily Show* exploded in popularity, other shows followed, most notably *The Colbert Report*—in which host Stephen Colbert played a conservative character and pretended to be outraged at the liberal media—and *Last Week Tonight with John Oliver*, another news entertainment show.

As many cable news producers have learned, providing Americans with a fair and balanced interpretation of the news is proving difficult and isn't always welcomed by cable viewers. In fact, up until January 2017, Fox News's slogan was "Fair and Balanced," but that was later replaced with "Most Watched, Most Trusted," then with "Real News. Real Honest Opinion," which many people believed was the network's way of admitting it was biased. However, Fox News executives stated the decision had nothing to do with its programming and was simply a marketing strategy. Judging by the ratings racked up by MSNBC and Fox News, it seems Americans prefer their cable news served with strong doses of opinion, drama, and bias.

Yellow Journalism in the 21st Century

This kind of polarization and dramatic coverage of events is far from being a new phenomenon. In the 19th century, rival New York City newspaper publishers Joseph Pulitzer and William Randolph Hearst were in a fierce competition for newspaper sales. Pulitzer's *New York World* featured a popular cartoon drawn by Richard F. Outcault called Hogan's Alley that included

John Oliver was sued by Bob Murray, the executive of a coal company, after Oliver made several jokes at Murray's expense on his show while truthfully describing several unethical actions Murray had taken. The lawsuit was later dismissed because of the right to free speech and a free press in the United States.

a character called the Yellow Kid. Recognizing the value of the cartoon, Hearst hired Outcault to work for his *New York Journal*. The resulting profit-driven conflict for the Yellow Kid led to the term yellow journalism.

Yellow journalism refers to the sensationalized, or biased and exaggerated, reporting of world events as a way to increase profits. At this time, the island of Cuba was a colony in the Spanish Empire. Cuba had been home to a growing revolutionary movement for several decades, and the United States was pressuring the Spanish to withdraw from the island. Pulitzer and Hearst focused a great deal of attention on the conflict, publishing dramatic headlines, exaggerated stories of Spanish cruelty, and tales of the heroic revolutionaries. Accuracy and impartiality were forgotten in the pursuit of sales and profit.

In an attempt to resolve tensions between the United States and Spain, the US Navy sent a battleship, the USS *Maine*, to Havana harbor in Cuba. However, on February 15, 1898, an explosion sank and destroyed the *Maine*. While witnesses and a report by the Cuban government agreed the explosion occurred on the ship, Hearst instead spread rumors of a plot to sink the ship. The misreporting of events capitalized on anti-Spanish feelings shared by politicians and the public alike. When a US investigation declared the *Maine* was destroyed by a mine in the harbor, the yellow journalists called for war. Within a few months, the United States followed through on those calls, leading to the Spanish-American War.

While the events surrounding the sinking of the *Maine* actually occurred and anti-Spanish feelings had existed for some time, the public perception and reaction to them was significant. By reporting in this sensationalized manner, the press was able to manipulate the public perception of international events. Instead of a peaceful resolution to an unfortunate incident, escalating outrage led to war.

Yellow journalism and fake news are very similar, although yellow journalism is intended mainly to attract viewers, while fake news is intended mainly to influence public opinion on

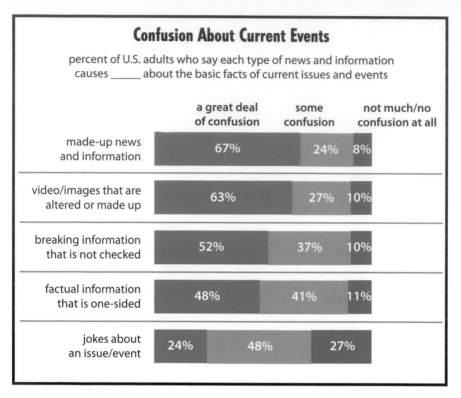

Confusion About Current Events

percent of U.S. adults who say each type of news and information causes _____ about the basic facts of current issues and events

	a great deal of confusion	some confusion	not much/no confusion at all
made-up news and information	67%	24%	8%
video/images that are altered or made up	63%	27%	10%
breaking information that is not checked	52%	37%	10%
factual information that is one-sided	48%	41%	11%
jokes about an issue/event	24%	48%	27%

Most Americans think fake news causes a lot of confusion about what's really happening in the world, as this information from the Pew Research Center shows. Many believe bias does as well.

an issue. Yellow journalism is more accurately compared to modern clickbait, or sensationalized headlines meant to get people to click on an article. As with cable news networks, websites aim to attract viewers, which is why they use clickbait. The more views a website gets, the more money the people behind it make. This tends to make some websites less concerned with truth and accuracy and more concerned with entertainment that appeals to people's sense of curiosity or outrage.

Clickbait titles themselves tend to be misleading or downright false, but many people share them on social media without reading the actual articles. As social media has become a common source of news about current events, Americans are encountering more inaccurate or unverified news stories every day. In the wake of the 2016 presidential election, the Pew Research Center found that 64 percent of Americans believed fake news stories have been causing a great deal of confusion and misinformation about current events and the facts surrounding them. This rose to 67 percent in 2019. Although it's difficult to determine how much fake news people are seeing, the perception that these stories are damaging is widely agreed upon.

Americans also agree that action must be taken to prevent the spread of misleading fake news stories. Many respondents to the Pew poll wanted the government and elected officials to prevent the spread of misinformation. They also wanted social media websites and internet search engines to take action against fake news stories. Most also agreed that the public was partially responsible for preventing made-up stories from being spread. While more than 80 percent of individuals surveyed believed they were able to identify fake news stories, nearly 23 percent admitted that they had knowingly or unknowingly shared a story that was fake.

Mainstream vs. Alternative

Widely known and generally credible news sources are known as the "mainstream media." These news outlets all tend to report the news as it happens, which means they report generally the same story but may put a biased spin on it, depending on whether the news outlet leans left or right. In contrast, the "alternative media" consists of websites that model themselves after news outlets. They often present stories that aren't backed up by facts and claim that the mainstream media doesn't want people to know about them. This is a dangerous claim because it makes it impossible to tell which stories are being ignored by other media outlets because they don't fit a particular narrative and which are being overlooked because they simply aren't true. Alternative media websites are often fake news, but they accuse the mainstream media of being the one that's fake.

One alternative media source that has repeatedly been proven false is Infowars. This website, run by Alex Jones, frequently presents conspiracy theories as if they're fact, and Jones is known

Alex Jones is known for his angry rants about things he claims the mainstream media wants to hide.

for getting extremely angry and ranting about them at length. John Oliver called him "a charismatic performer who gets charged up on a regular basis."[5] In one widely known example, Jones falsely reported that the armed forces were putting chemicals into drinking water in an attempt to turn enemies of the United States gay. Jones yelled while hitting his desk, "What do you think tap water is? It's a gay bomb, baby ... You think I am, like, shocked by it so I'm up here bashing it because I don't like gay people? I don't like them putting chemicals in the water that turn the ... frogs gay! Do you understand that?"[6] Jones's anger often strikes a chord with viewers, despite the fact that he's getting angry over things that are frequently proven to be untrue. Infowars is well known for publishing fake news stories and has been banned from multiple social media platforms, including YouTube, Twitter, and Facebook.

In December 2019, a former Infowars employee named Josh Owens wrote an article for the *New York Times* about what it was like to work for Jones. He described several instances in which he and his coworkers were ordered to make up stories that would generate interest in Infowars. Owens described the incident that eventually made him reevaluate the work he had been doing:

> I made my way to upstate New York on assignment, along with a reporter and second cameraman. We were sent to visit Muslim-majority communities throughout the United States to investigate what Jones instructed us to call "the American Caliphate [Muslim political leader or regime]" ...
>
> We landed in Newark at 12:30 p.m. on December 1, 2015. The first stop was Islamberg, a Muslim community three hours north of Manhattan ... unfounded rumors circulated around far-right corners of the internet that this community was a potential terrorist-training center ... Because of the conspiracy theories about the place, Islamberg was a constant target of right-wing extremists ... So the phone call we received later that night from a law-enforcement agent shouldn't have come as a sur-

Fake News Is Not Satire

Satire is a type of writing that uses exaggeration and sarcasm to make a point in a humorous way, but many people have difficulty telling the difference between fake news and satire. Sometimes this is because the satirical articles are not written well. If they're too close to the truth or sound too much like something a reasonable person might say, the humor won't come through. Some websites that publish satirical articles do this on purpose to confuse people. Other times, people can't tell the difference because they're unfamiliar with satire.

One way to tell the difference between the two is to check which website an article is coming from. Some well-known satirical websites are The Onion, Clickhole, Reductress, and Above Average. These websites never post anything completely truthful, but sometimes people are fooled into thinking that what they're reading is serious. Occasionally, even the real news networks are fooled by a satirical story and feature it on their shows. For instance, The Onion posted an article in 2004 titled "Study: 58 Percent of U.S. Exercise Televised." According to *HuffPost*:

> *Deborah Norville stated on her MSNBC show that a new study said that 58 percent of exercise done in America was on broadcast television. Whoever wrote the script that night literally wrote, "For instance, of the 3.5 billion sit-ups done during 2003, two million, 30,000 of them were on exercise shows on Lifetime or one of the ESPN channels," [a clearly sarcastic joke from the article] as if it were news copy.*[1]

Most satirical news websites will state that they're satire. If you're unsure about whether something you're reading is satire or not, think about whether the story sounds like a joke or contains information that doesn't seem possible to verify. If you're still unsure, do a search to see if any other news outlets are reporting the same story independently.

1. "17 Times 'The Onion' Fooled People Who Should Know Better (PICTURES)," *HuffPost*, modified September 26, 2012, www.huffpost.com/entry/fooled-by-the-onion_n_1912413?slideshow=true#gallery/5bad08dde4b04234e8560795/8.

prise. The officer who contacted us said he simply wanted to verify who we were after receiving a concerned call from someone in Islamberg. We told Jones about it, and he chose to believe it was a veiled threat ...

Jones told us to file a story that accused the police of harassment, lending credence [believability] to the theory that this community contained dangerous, potential terrorists. I knew this wasn't the case according to the information we had. We all did. Days before, we spoke to the sheriff and the mayor of ... a nearby municipality. They both told us the people in Islamberg were kind, generous neighbors who welcomed the surrounding community into their homes, even celebrating holidays together. The information did not meet our expectations, so we made it up, preying on the vulnerable and feeding the prejudices and fears of Jones's audience.[7]

Later, thinking about how scary life must be for the people—especially the children—who lived in Islamberg, Owens started to realize that what he was doing wasn't right. By sharing false stories, Infowars was putting real people's lives in danger from those who believed the fake news. He soon found another job and took it even though it paid much less than Jones had been paying him.

Developing Media Literacy

Staying informed about fake news and the blurred lines between entertainment and journalism is an important part of developing media literacy skills. Following the 2016 US presidential election, Facebook released the following guidelines:

1. *Be skeptical of headlines. False news stories often have catchy headlines in all caps with exclamation points. If shocking claims in the headline sound unbelievable, they probably are.*

2. *Look closely at the URL. A phony or look-alike URL may be a warning sign of false news. Many false news sites mimic authentic news sources by making small changes*

to the URL. You can go to the site to compare the URL to established sources.

3. **Investigate the source.** *Ensure that the story is written by a source that you trust with a reputation for accuracy. If the story comes from an unfamiliar organization, check their "About" section to learn more.*

4. **Watch for unusual formatting.** *Many false news sites have misspellings or awkward layouts. Read carefully if you see these signs.*

5. **Consider the photos.** *False news stories often contain manipulated images or videos. Sometimes the photo may be authentic, but taken out of context. You can search for the photo or image to verify where it came from.*

6. **Inspect the dates.** *False news stories may contain timelines that make no sense, or event dates that have been altered.*

7. **Check the evidence.** *Check the author's sources to confirm that they are accurate. Lack of evidence or reliance on unnamed experts may indicate a false news story.*

8. **Look at other reports.** *If no other news source is reporting the same story, it may indicate that the story is false. If the story is reported by multiple sources you trust, it's more likely to be true.*

9. **Is the story a joke?** *Sometimes false news stories can be hard to distinguish from humor or satire. Check whether the source is known for parody, and whether the story's details and tone suggest it may be just for fun.*

10. *Some stories are intentionally false.* *Think critically about the stories you read, and only share news that you know to be credible.*[8]

These guidelines help inform readers of how to spot fake news stories and empower them to think critically about the information they're being presented with. Additionally, CBS News released a list of 22 fake news websites that are designed to look like real news outlets, including Infowars, 70News, *World News Report*, the *Boston Tribune*, the *Christian Times*, and more. Some are deliberately spreading false information, while others are doing so by accident, and still others are intended to be satire. One website, called Newslo, has both factual and satirical stories on its website, which makes it difficult at times for readers to tell what's true and what's not. Developing media literacy skills makes it easier for viewers to spot outright fake news as well as modern yellow journalism and clickbait, whether it's on the internet or on a cable news network.

Your Opinion Matters!

1. In what ways have cable news networks blurred the lines between news and entertainment?

2. Why is fake news dangerous?

3. How confident do you feel in your ability to identify fake news? Explain your answer.

CHAPTER THREE

NEWS ON
THE INTERNET

The rise of the internet has forever changed the way people get their news. Most newspapers have moved online, and news channels can upload video or stream it live to give people breaking updates. News articles can gain widespread attention if they go viral. However, increased access to the internet has also caused problems. Because anyone can write a blog or upload a video, the amount of fake news available has exploded. Anyone can make up anything and put it online, and they frequently do so with clickbait headlines promising to tell people the "truth" that the mainstream media has been hiding from them. Tricks such as video manipulation and staging, or setting up a situation to be photographed and circulated, have become common. An example of staging is when people who support a certain cause sometimes show up at protests against that cause specifically to create trouble and portray the protesters as violent and untrustworthy, thereby decreasing public support for them. An example of photo editing was revealed in 2018, when a government photographer admitted to editing photos of Donald Trump's inauguration to make the crowd look bigger. As trust in the mainstream media declines, these fake news websites gain more followers.

Photos such as this one have been shared on social media for years. People claim the fruit is called a moon melon, and some people sell "moon melon seeds" on Amazon. Many people have been fooled by this photoshopped picture of a watermelon. Moon melons do not exist.

Blogs Blend Facts with Opinions

As blogs started dominating the internet, liberal and conservative activists realized the potential of the medium to spread their messages. Soon, they established their own websites to report both the news and their opinion of it. Not all of them are fake news websites, but many allow much more biased reporting than traditional news outlets do. On the left, among the most popular websites are *HuffPost*, Politico, Slate, and *Daily Kos*. On the right, a familiar complaint has prompted readers to seek out conservative bloggers: The mainstream media is too liberal and doesn't reflect their ideas and values, so they have chosen to go elsewhere for their news. Some of the most popular conservative blogs and websites include Breitbart, American Thinker, Townhall, and the *Federalist*.

As more and more reputable news sources feature their own blog sections, including the *New York Times* and the *Washington Post*, it is getting increasingly difficult for readers to tell what is a legitimate news source and what is opinion-based, biased reporting. This is especially true when people title their blogs in a way that mimics longstanding newspapers; for example, putting words such as "news," "post," "gazette," and "times" in their name. Unfortunately there is not yet an easy solution to this problem; currently it's up to the reader to investigate multiple news sources in order to form their own opinion instead of automatically believing everything they read.

According to the BBC, some fake news websites are motivated by fun and profit. Allen Montgomery, the founder of a website called The National Report, which intentionally publishes fake stories, said, "There are highs that you get from watching traffic spikes and kind of baiting people into the story. I just find it to be a lot of fun."[1] The BBC added that "there is big money to be made from sites by The National Report which host web advertising, and these potentially huge rewards entice website owners to move away from funny satirical jokes and towards more believable content because it is likely to be more widely shared."[2] When people are outraged by something, they tend to share it on

Trump and Fake News

Donald Trump has repeatedly criticized news sources that run negative stories about him. He frequently calls such coverage fake news, even when there is a clear record that the things they're reporting are true. A database of Trump's public remarks contained 320 references to fake news in 2017 alone. In one instance that took place in February 2020, a photographer snapped and later tweeted a picture of Trump walking across the White House lawn. With the wind blowing his hair back, the tan line on his face was clearly visible. After the photo went viral, Trump tweeted, "More Fake News. This was photoshopped, obviously, but the wind was strong and the hair looks good? Anything to demean!"[1] The photographer whose photo went viral admitted to using an app to enhance the orange color of Trump's face. However, other photos taken by other photographers on the same day show the same tan line.

Trump has also spread fake news himself. In May 2017, Trump tweeted about an investigation into his ties to Russia, stating that former Director of National Intelligence James Clapper "reiterated what everybody, including the fake media already knows—there is 'no evidence' of collusion w/Russia and Trump."[2] FactCheck.org explained, "This is an example of Trump passing along false information, while criticizing the 'fake media.' Trump misquoted ... Clapper."[3] The president has demonstrated many times that he does such things on purpose. In July 2016, when Trump was still campaigning for the Republican presidential nomination, CBS reporter Lesley Stahl asked him off-camera why he kept saying negative things about the media. According to Stahl and a nearby witness, he responded, "You know why I do it? I do it to discredit you all and demean you all so when you write negative stories about me no one will believe you."[4]

1. Donald Trump (@realDonaldTrump), "More Fake News," Twitter, February 8, 2020, 2:13 p.m., twitter.com/realdonaldtrump/status/1226222654019035142.

2. Donald Trump (@realDonaldTrump), "Director Clapper reiterated," Twitter, May 8, 2017, 3:41 p.m., twitter.com/realDonaldTrump/status/861712617299210240.

3. Eugene Kiely, "Trump's Phony 'Fake News' Claims," FactCheck.org, January 16, 2018, www.factcheck.org/2018/01/trumps-phony-fake-news-claims.

4. Quoted in Bernard Goldberg, "The Worst Thing About Trump's 'Fake News' Warning," The Hill, November 11, 2019, thehill.com/opinion/white-house/469408-the-worst-thing-about-trumps-fake-news-warning.

social media. According to Montgomery, some of the stories on The National Report have earned as much as $10,000 because of how much they were shared.

The Good and the Bad of Blogs

By the early years of the 21st century, it was estimated that about 500,000 active blogs were on the internet, including many devoted to politics and other issues found in the news. Bloggers soon proved themselves resourceful journalists, finding stories ignored by the mainstream media. For example, in 2016, an oil pipeline called the Dakota Access Pipeline (DAPL) was proposed to run through the Standing Rock Indian Reservation. Many Native Americans who lived on the reservation protested the DAPL because if the pipeline ever leaked, it would pollute their drinking water. The DAPL affected a relatively small group of people, so most news networks never mentioned the protest at first. It became a national movement after people shared pictures and videos of the protest on Facebook and blogs. After finding out about it, many people donated money, food, and other materials to help keep the protest going. With more people paying attention, major news networks began covering it, but people still relied on live videos posted to Facebook to show them what was really happening, including some unethical police tactics, as these were generally left out of the mainstream news coverage. The coverage of this story earned the protesters a victory: The administration of then-president Barack Obama refused to issue a permit that was needed for the DAPL to be built. However, the victory was short-lived. A few months later, after he took office, Donald Trump reversed the decision, and the pipeline was built. As the protesters predicted, the pipeline leaked and caused environmental damage.

While blogging can enable citizen journalists to use the powers of the internet to uncover news, blogging is at its worst when bloggers act irresponsibly—spreading rumors, misinformation, and biases online. Since there is often no editor to make sure that what they publish on their websites is fair, balanced, and accurate, bloggers can sometimes be unethical.

Many news outlets didn't start reporting on the Standing Rock protests (*shown here*) until they had gone viral on social media.

Some blogs are little more than long and rambling rants by anonymous bloggers whose entries contain numerous typographical errors as well as misspellings and misuses of grammar and punctuation—and if they can't get the spelling or punctuation right, chances are the bloggers aren't getting their facts straight, either. However, this doesn't mean that a blog with perfect spelling and grammar will be completely accurate. Poor writing is simply one hint that an article doesn't come from a reputable source.

Health scares are a good example of how blogging can quickly get out of control. Many people report rumors on their blogs that are spread through social media such as Facebook and Twitter, as well as other blogs, which makes the effect much worse.

The news spreads so fast that people read the same rumor multiple times on multiple websites, not realizing that all these websites are taking their news from each other. One example was the Ebola scare in the United States in 2014. Ebola is a deadly disease, but it's very hard to catch. It isn't spread through the air; someone must come into direct contact with the bodily fluid of an infected person who is showing symptoms. However, when a few people in the United States were found to have Ebola, many news outlets reported this as if the disease was going to spread like wildfire and kill everyone in the country. Some bloggers added fuel to the fire by spreading claims that were completely false. *Forbes* magazine reported some of the wildest online rumors:

> *Did you read the one about the Ebola victims who have risen from the dead to become zombies? Or the reported cases of the disease in California, Kansas City and the Bahamas? ...*
>
> *Take a little wander through the more obscure corners of the internet, and you'll discover that Ebola is airborne, it can only be destroyed by nuclear warheads, and the US government is planning to build death camps to intern the millions of victims who are inevitably going to come down with the disease. Either that, of course, or it's a bio-warfare weapon created by the US with Africa being used as a test laboratory ...*
>
> *More dangerously, drinking salt water has been claimed online to cure the disease, killing two people in Nigeria and hospitalizing dozens more.*[3]

Elizabeth Osder, leader of an internet business strategy group called the Osder Group, said blogs consist of "opinion without expertise, without resources, without reporting."[4] While this may not be true of all blogs, it's certainly true of many of them. As the readership statistics for some of the top blogs indicate, though, many people seem to prefer their news with a little bias. Rather than finding fair, accurate, and unbiased reporting, they find bloggers who speak directly to their passions and prejudices. Additionally, the interactive nature of blogs attracts many readers;

people like to be able to respond to what they're reading, whether they support or oppose it.

Students seeking to gather research for school projects may encounter the same biases and limited backgrounds on the internet as consumers of news. It may be difficult for students to detect bias in what they're reading, making it harder for them to find the answers they need. A book that explores all sides of a complicated issue may be a much more appropriate method of researching a topic than trying to pull together a string of facts from a variety of biased or misleading websites.

A 2016 study by Stanford University found that about 82 percent of students have difficulty telling the difference between legitimate news stories, ads that are sponsored by companies to promote a certain point or product, and news articles that are intentionally misleading. In one example, an article about toxic waste near a Japanese nuclear plant was accompanied by a picture of deformed flowers. Although there was no citation for the picture, many students who viewed the article believed, based on the headline, that the picture provided proof of the article's claims.

Some experts have offered tips to help young adults become more media literate. An article in the *Wall Street Journal* advised teachers:

> Rather than trusting the "about" section of a website to learn about it, teach them "lateral reading"—leaving the website almost immediately after landing on it and research the organization or author. Also, explain to teens that a top ranking on Google doesn't mean an article is trustworthy. The rankings are based on several factors, including popularity.

> Students should learn to evaluate sources' reliability based on whether they're named, independent and well-informed or authoritative, says Jonathan Anzalone, assistant director of the Center for News Literacy at Stony Brook University in New York. Posts should cite multiple sources, and the information should be verifiable elsewhere, he says.[5]

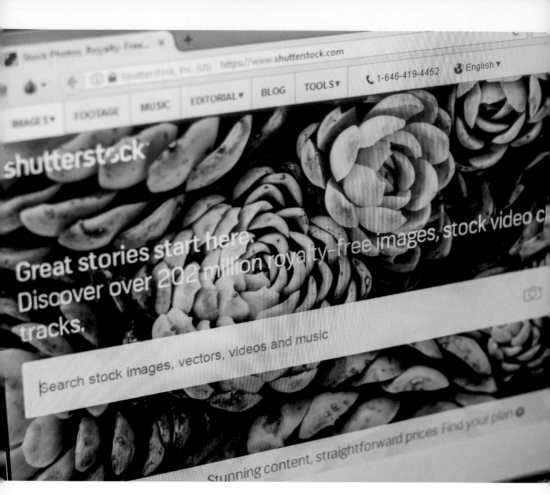

Many websites use stock photos—pictures anyone can buy, such as those found on the website Shutterstock—to illustrate their articles. This doesn't prove the content in the article is false, but readers shouldn't automatically assume a photo proves an article's claims true.

Many young adults are also unaware that sponsored content is generally a less trustworthy source of information. In 2014, John Oliver reported on the problem of advertising and the news. Many news outlets rely on advertising to help them make enough money to do things such as pay their staff and pay for web hosting. However, this can sometimes create media bias. For instance, online newspapers are increasingly using a tactic called native advertising to attract companies. This involves disguising an ad as a legitimate news article so more people will click on it. The ads generally have small disclaimers at the top or bottom such as "sponsored content," then make a point that helps sell the advertiser's service or product.

Some people see no problem with native advertising because of the disclaimers. However, as Oliver pointed out, "it is a problem though, because the consumer cannot tell the difference. A recent study showed that less than half of visitors to a news site could distinguish between native advertising and actual news. And of course they can't! Because it's supposed to blend in."[6]

In addition to causing confusion among readers, native advertising can compromise a news outlet's other content. As an example, Oliver discussed an article published in *The Atlantic* that was sponsored by the Church of Scientology and was highly complimentary of the group and its leader. For people who were aware that this was an advertisement, this made it difficult for them to trust *The Atlantic*'s other articles. However, for those who were fooled into thinking it was true journalism, it may have had a different negative effect. Reading such a positive article in a news source that is generally considered trustworthy may have made people believe only positive things about the Church of Scientology. If they read anything negative in a later article, even if it's published in a different trustworthy news source or in another article in *The Atlantic*, they may discount the facts in the second article because they go against the beliefs the person has already formed. This is why it's important for everyone—teens as well as adults—to be critical of what they read and examine both the source and any potential sponsors.

Going Viral

The spread of news on social media has also caused a lot of misinformation to circulate, and it can be very difficult to know what's real and what's not. For example, in 2020, Iran fired missiles at two US military bases in Iraq after a US drone attack killed a high-ranking Iranian general named Qassem Soleimani. Soon after news of the Iranian missile attacks broke, social media users

Breaking News on Social Media

Over the years, social media websites have become an increasingly popular source of information about current events. Many official institutions maintain at least one type of account, and various news organizations and reporters frequently post stories on these accounts. However, it's not only news outlets sharing important stories; anyone can view or share a post, and information can spread quickly this way.

In 2018, the Pew Research Center reported that 50 percent of internet users get their news from social media before they hear anything about it on a news channel. Many people then go from social media to a news website to get a clearer picture of what's happening. However, many others simply read the headline and keep scrolling. Furthermore, the way social media websites work limits what kind of news someone sees. In an article for *Forbes* magazine, Nicole Martin explained:

> *An article needs to be "liked" and shared multiple times before many people see it in their feed. Therefore social media and your social friends have control over what news pieces you see and what you do not. There are also many "fake news" websites that compete for attention with sensational headlines and ridiculous storylines that tend to get shared more often due to the lack of readers fact checking or reading more than the headline ... In fact, fake news is actually more likely to spread than the truth.*[1]

The downside of having social media break news stories to people is that news networks often feel pressured to keep up, which can lead to poorly researched stories that need to be corrected later. Additionally, some people feel social media posts are more trustworthy than news outlets. People with this view believe—often falsely—that people sharing things on social media have no need to put a biased spin on the news the way some news outlets do. In reality, most things that are shared on social media are trying to convince people of something.

1. Nicole Martin, "How Social Media Has Changed How We Consume News," *Forbes*, November 30, 2018, www.forbes.com/sites/nicolemartin1/2018/11/30/how-social-media-has-changed-how-we-consume-news.

started sharing photos and videos designed to mislead people. NBC News mentioned a few such incidents:

> *A Twitter user responded … to a tweet from President Donald Trump with an image purported [claimed] to be Ain al-Asad air base under attack. The image was actually from an incident in the Gaza Strip, which borders Israel, in November … Similarly, an image showing Iran's supreme leader, Ayatollah Ali Khamenei … circulated online … It was purported to show Khamenei supervising the attack on Ain al-Asad, but it appears to be an edited version of an image released by Iran in 2014 during an Islamic*

Protests such as this one erupted after a US drone strike killed Qassem Soleimani. These fueled American fears of retaliation, and with tensions running high, many people shared images online without stopping to check if their descriptions were accurate.

Revolutionary Guard Corps exhibition … In addition to errone-
ous photos and videos that have been shared online, a number of
social media accounts posted false claims that Iraq had declared
war on the United States, as well as reports of U.S. casualties
in Tuesday's attacks, which Trump denied in an address to the
nation Wednesday.[7]

Some people share things without realizing they're false. Others do it deliberately to mislead people into forming certain opinions. In one example, Republican representative Paul Gosar tweeted a picture of Barack Obama shaking hands with the Iranian president. In reality, someone had photoshopped a 2011 image of Obama shaking hands with the former prime minister of India, putting the Iranian president's head on the prime minister's body. When people informed Gosar of this, he defended his tweet by saying, "No one said this wasn't photoshopped."[8] However, knowingly sharing a photoshopped image without explaining that it's fake is a form of deception and contributes to the spread of fake news.

These incidents are certainly not the first problems social media websites have had regarding the spread of fake news. After the 2016 US presidential election, it started to become clear that Russia had influenced the results, mainly by spreading fake news through fake social media profiles. On May 17, 2017, former FBI director Robert Mueller was appointed by the Justice Department to look into allegations of Russian interference in the Trump campaign. Mueller was assisted by 19 lawyers, 40 FBI agents, and a team of financial and intelligence analysts. Nearly 3,000 court appearances and 500 witnesses later, Mueller released a 448-page report on April 18, 2019. The report stated Russian interference had indeed occurred through the creation of fake social media accounts. Other researchers found after the election that the Russian government had "created and spread misleading articles online with the goal of punishing Democrat Hillary Clinton, helping Republican Donald Trump and undermining faith in American democracy."[9] An investigation into the matter found that although the Russians likely didn't actively change people's votes—for example, by hacking voting machines—their fake news campaign did help sway voters to Trump's side and accomplished its goal of making Americans suspicious of news outlets. According to *TIME* magazine, "Throughout 2016, [Russian trolls] posted divisive content about topics such as Black Lives Matter, immigration and gun control; they bought political ads criticizing Clinton; and they pumped out hashtags like #Hillary4Prison and #TrumpTrain to their masses of followers."[10]

People read these posts and shared them with their own followers, helping the Russians reach a wider audience than they could have alone. In one example, which came to be known as Pizzagate, Russian trolls, people who were connected to the Trump campaign, and unknown social media users started spreading rumors that Clinton was involved in running a sex trafficking ring, selling underage girls into slavery to billionaires. This was supposedly being done in secret in the basement of a pizza restaurant called Comet Ping Pong in Washington, DC. Infowars and Breitbart picked up the story and exaggerated it; for instance, Alex Jones added a claim of satanic rituals to the story of sexual abuse. A North Carolina man named Edgar Maddison Welch became so convinced of these stories that he brought two guns and a knife to Comet Ping Pong, ready to free the captive children. He found no children, and he also found that the restaurant doesn't even have a basement. His actions proved beyond a doubt that the rumors were false, but they also proved how dangerous fake news can be, as he could have seriously hurt or killed someone with the weapons he brought to the restaurant.

Because of incidents such as this one, people have started calling for social media websites to take a more active role in finding and removing fake news from their platforms. In response to such criticisms, many social media websites have promised to do so. However, many of their plans have been criticized as meaningless or ineffective. For example, although Facebook has announced its intention to monitor and remove fake content, the number of posts that are made on the platform makes it impossible for them to catch everything. They rely heavily on people

In 2016, many people became convinced that the Pizzagate scandal was real. Although it was entirely made up, this strongly held belief hurt Hillary Clinton's presidential campaign.

to report such content, but if someone is fooled by a post, they aren't going to report it. A good answer has yet to be found; until it is, social media users must be very skeptical of what they read online and shouldn't share anything they haven't personally attempted to verify.

Your Opinion Matters!

1. Why are news stories reported in blogs given less credibility than stories reported in newspapers and magazines?

2. How has the internet enabled readers to become active participants as news gatherers and commentators?

3. What are some actions you should take before sharing something you read online?

TARGETS OF BIAS

When people talk about bias in the media, they most frequently mean political bias that promotes the political views of a certain party. However, there are all kinds of bias. Just as with political bias, these other types can sometimes have dangerous consequences for their targets. Sometimes the bias is obvious, but other times it's so subtle that people can be influenced by it without even realizing it.

Gender, Sexuality, and Bias

Many people hold a conscious or unconscious bias against women, especially in areas that have traditionally been dominated by men. These include STEM fields, business, and politics. For instance, Dr. Erika Falk, chief operating officer and program director of the Israel Institute, examined the media coverage of eight presidential campaigns and found that male candidates were the subject of twice as many stories as female candidates and that the stories written about male candidates were generally longer. Moreover, she said, the stories about the male candidates focused far more often on their positions on policies, whereas the stories about women tended to focus more on their personalities, backgrounds,

One way the media tends to show gender bias is in entertainment reporting. Male celebrities are often asked questions about how they do their work, while women who do the same jobs are more frequently asked questions about their diet and wardrobe.

and families. According to Falk, the gender bias found in the media coverage of presidential campaigns has an impact that goes beyond that year's presidential race. By not treating women as equal competitors for the presidency, she said, the press plays a role in maintaining the male domination of politics. She said fewer women are encouraged to enter politics because they find fewer role models holding high political office.

This gender bias was evident during Hillary Clinton's presidential campaigns. Despite the obstacles faced by women in politics, then-senator Hillary Clinton of New York managed to break into the top tier of candidates competing for the presidency in the 2008 election. Still, Clinton found herself fighting against gender bias in the media. According to Falk, when Clinton announced her candidacy, 36 major daily newspapers covered the event and published stories. At the time, Falk said, then-senator Barack Obama of Illinois was trailing well behind Clinton in the polls. However, when Obama announced his candidacy, 59 major daily newspapers covered the story. Falk said the bias shown in the Clinton-Obama race was simply another case of the press focusing more on male candidates.

Other observers believe the bias against Clinton went beyond the news columns of daily newspapers—that Clinton was also treated unfairly by other media, particularly the cable TV commentators who often criticized her clothing and appearance. Her relationship with her husband, former president Bill Clinton, was also the subject of jokes. Bill had been unfaithful to Hillary during his presidency, and many people seemed to falsely believe this was a reflection of her presidential abilities. After Clinton won the 2008 New Hampshire primary, Bill Kristol, editor of the conservative *Weekly Standard*, suggested that female voters cast their ballots for Clinton out of sympathy or support for a fellow woman rather than because they agreed with her positions on the economy, health care, and other important issues.

Such comments by male journalists reinforced the opinions many people hold about gender bias in the media—that even when a prominent woman steps forward and wins a hotly contested race, male journalists can be counted on to attribute the win to factors that have nothing to do with her ability to govern. "Sen. Hillary Clinton's run for the Democratic nomination has been fraught with sexism, exposing an ugly streak within the American press," media critic Jessica Wakeman wrote. "Degrading ... attacks on Clinton spanned from print to radio, from the Web to television."[1] Clinton faced similar problems in the 2016 presidential race. For instance, after one debate between Trump and Clinton, Fox News host Brit Hume described the candidates differently:

> Hume ... described Trump as looking "annoyed" and "put out," but the host didn't stop there. He added that Clinton seemed "composed,

Many people view the same behavior differently depending on whether it comes from a man or woman. Women who yell or look stern are often mocked, while men who do the same are often respected.

smug sometimes," but "not necessarily attractive." Hume later clarified that he was "talking about demeanor." On social media, many were quick to point out that Hume said nothing about Trump's attractiveness, but was quick to critique Clinton's debate performance alongside her physical attractiveness.[2]

Another way the media can be biased against women is by ignoring them in favor of men. In an article published in 2016,

Hard to Spot

Some examples of bias are obvious, but others are very subtle and easy to miss. One source of subtle bias is the words an author chooses. Accuracy in Media (AIM), a group that points out instances of liberal media bias, gave one example:

Which version sounds less biased to you?

A. *"Heart-wrenching tales of hardship faced by people whose care is dependent on Medicaid"*
B. *"Information on the lifestyles of Medicaid dependents" ...*

Everyone who uses words is guilty of using biased word choice—even those writers out there who consciously attempt to use neutral language. That's because everyone has a unique worldview, and that worldview tends to express itself whether obvious or not.[1]

Being aware of this type of bias can help readers and viewers spot it and decide whether or not they agree with a reporter's word choice and worldview.

Another example of subtle bias is the types of photos that are shown alongside a story. For instance, during the 2016 presidential election, news outlets that were left-leaning would generally show pictures that made Clinton look professional and Trump look angry, while right-leaning news outlets often showed Trump looking dignified and Clinton looking silly.

Word choice and photo choice are often combined to pack an extra powerful punch. For instance, in 2015, two groups of men

Atlantic executive editor Adrienne LaFrance noted that "in newsrooms and in news articles, men ... make more money, get more bylines, spend more time on-camera, and are quoted far more often than women."[3] Part of the issue is that many of the people who are in positions of power—and therefore who do newsworthy things— are also men, due to this same gender bias. However, LaFrance pointed out that there was more to it than that. When she analyzed her own articles, she found that she was not

were arrested for burglary and both stories, written by the same journalist, were published in the Iowa newspaper the *Gazette*. The first group, three white men, were University of Iowa students who were on the wrestling team. They were described in terms of their accomplishments—"Three University of Iowa Wrestlers Arrested, Suspended"[2]—and their yearbook photos were published with the article. The second group consisted of four black men; the article mentioned that they had behaved violently, and instead of yearbook photos, their police mug shots were used. This difference made the group of white men look much more respectable than the group of black men. After the difference was pointed out on multiple other websites, the *Gazette* published the white men's mug shots as well as an explanation of its original photo choice.

The same thing has happened to victims of police violence; the police officer is generally shown smiling in uniform, while the victim—frequently a black man—is shown looking threatening. This has led to the viral hashtag #IfTheyGunnedMeDown, in which black people share two different photos of themselves side by side as a way to show that everyone, no matter their race, has different sides to their personality. The hashtag refers to black people questioning which photo the media would share if they were victimized: one in which they look respectable, or one in which they look silly or threatening?

1. Allie Duzett, "Media Bias in Strategic Word Choice," Accuracy in Media, April 28, 2011, www.aim.org/on-target-blog/media-bias-in-strategic-word-choice.

2. Lee Hermiston, "Three University of Iowa Wrestlers Arrested, Suspended," *Gazette*, modified April 3, 2015, www.thegazette.com/subject/news/three-university-of-iowa-wrestlers-arrested-20150324.

immune to this kind of bias, even though she knew it was common and tried to avoid it. In 2013, the first time she tried this experiment, she found that she mentioned women only 25 percent of the time. In 2015, that number decreased to 22 percent. LaFrance wrote that "by failing to quote or mention very many women, I'm one of the forces actively contributing to a world in which women's skills and accomplishments are undermined or ignored, and women are excluded."[4]

Some people, LaFrance said, argue that her work isn't to seek out sources that fit a specific characteristic but only to seek out sources that are the most qualified. However, she pointed out that there's no reason to assume a woman in a certain field would be any less qualified than a man; it's just easier to find men to quote. She decided to take the advice of Nathan Mathias, the PhD student who helped her analyze her data. Mathias suggested that LaFrance make an effort to intentionally seek out more newsworthy women, even though it might take a little more effort. Just because women are often overlooked in the media doesn't mean they aren't making contributions; finding and reporting on those contributions could help change the way women are viewed in society.

As with women, members of the LGBTQ+ community are often depicted poorly in the media. For example, in May 2009, *Esquire* magazine published a story that was intended to be funny, claiming to teach its largely male readership the proper ways in which to use profanity. In the story, though, the author used derogatory expressions for gay people. Pro-LGBTQ+ organization GLAAD responded quickly and issued a complaint with David Granger, *Esquire*'s editor at that time, who acknowledged that the magazine had done something wrong. In an apology published online and in the June issue, the magazine wrote, "The target of the parody was profanity itself and not the various people who might be its object, including gay people. But we used a particularly offensive phrase we shouldn't have. It certainly was not our intent to cause pain. Judging from the reaction, we did. For that we are sincerely sorry."[5]

The media coverage of 2020 presidential candidate Pete Buttigieg was one example of the bias LGBTQ+ people face. Buttigieg had been asked questions such as whether he was "gay enough" or "too gay," but his heterosexual opponents were never asked similar questions about their sexuality. Additionally, many news stories reported on Buttigieg in ways that were harmful to his candidacy. For example, the *New York Times* published a profile called "Pete Buttigieg's Life in the Closet," which talked about how Buttigieg publicly came out as gay. However, Leigh Moscowitz, author of *Media and the Coming Out of Gay Male Athletes in Team Sports*, said, "'The closet' implies secrecy, deception, and shame. And in a political realm where honesty and integrity are important, the characterization isn't helpful for a political candidate."[6] The *Columbia Journalism Review* further explained, "How LGBTQ candidates are perceived when they run for office is determined in large part by how the media treats their coming out stories, the historic nature of their candidacy, and their self-presentation. And the stories journalists report are shaped by ideas about sexual identity that are sometimes uninformed."[7]

Bias Against Religious Groups

Both right-leaning and left-leaning news sources have been accused of religious bias in their reporting. People who identify as conservative are often Christian, while people who identify as liberal generally represent a wider range of religious views. For this reason, right-leaning news sources are more likely to report stories of anti-Christian bias, while left-leaning ones are more likely to report bias against other religions. For instance, around December, conservative news outlets—particularly Fox News—frequently report about the "war on Christmas," which is a perceived attack on the holiday. The channel airs stories about companies wishing its customers "Happy Holidays" instead of "Merry Christmas" and point out Christmas merchandise that has a winter theme rather than a religious theme. In the view of people who believe there is a war on Christmas, Christians are being persecuted and prevented from celebrating their holiday. Liberal

As a gay man, presidential candidate Pete Buttigieg experienced a lot of bias in the way the news covered his candidacy.

news outlets often disagree with this view, stating that other religions are far more oppressed in Western society than Christianity is and that no one is preventing Christians themselves from saying "Merry Christmas" or using religious decorations.

On the other side of the spectrum, many liberal news outlets take issue with the media's reporting in regard to other religions, especially Islam. After a comment from a CNN anchor attacking the Muslim community in general, *HuffPost* wrote:

> *It's not just the fear-mongers at Fox News, who exploit terrorist attacks to fuel anti-Muslim hostility with such consistency it's almost not worth commenting on. It's the mainstream media, and while Islamophobia rears its head in print as well as online, it is most pronounced on television ...*

> *"Journalists, especially TV journalists, love scoops," says Nathan Lean, a scholar at Georgetown University's Prince Alwaleed bin Talal Center for Muslim-Christian Understanding. "So what happens is a lot of them ask leading questions—they insinuate, infer, hypothesize: 'Could it have been an attack carried out by Al-Qaeda?' Then all of a sudden the conversation is dominated by Al-Qaeda."*[8]

This is one way media bias is responsible for the spread of misinformation. Many people may see the first few reports after an incident, in which the media questions whether certain groups are to blame, and take those as factual reports. Later, when the truth is reported, those same people may either not see the broadcast or assume the second report is the false one.

Working to Expose Bias

One way to get the media's attention is to form watchdog groups such as GLAAD, which can organize members of minority communities to stage boycotts and similar activities. Minority groups have also found another effective strategy for dealing with media bias: They simply go into the media business themselves. There are news websites run by women, people of color, and LGBTQ+

The way the media reports on the Muslim community often makes it seem scary. In reality, the majority of Muslims are just regular people.

people. These websites cover stories that are of interest to these groups but may be ignored by the mainstream media. For example, the *Native Times* is one of the few news outlets to report on issues that affect Native Americans—a group that is largely ignored by the mainstream media.

By establishing their own newspapers and other media outlets, members of minority groups have been able to provide news coverage of the activities in their communities free of the biases they often find in the mainstream media. Indeed, the bias in the mainstream press—especially against people of color—was so deep that for many years big city newspapers and other important media outlets failed to report one of the major stories of the 20th century: the blossoming civil rights movement. It wasn't until the black press began accurately and fairly reporting African Americans' growing resentment toward their status as second-class citizens that the mainstream media finally recognized the importance of the story.

In the United States, people of color have a long history of establishing newspapers, radio stations, and magazines, in many cases specifically because they didn't believe their issues were covered fairly in the mainstream press. The first black-owned newspaper, *Freedom's Journal*, was established in New York City in 1827. It was founded specifically to counter the proslavery positions published in white-owned papers. From the 1890s through the early 1920s, while white-owned newspapers rarely reported the lynchings, or murders, of black people, the black-owned press published vivid accounts of the killings.

Following World War II, the black press covered the growing civil rights movement in America, editorializing strongly for equality. During the 1950s, as the civil rights movement turned into a huge story, the mainstream media discovered that its news staffs were overwhelmingly white and that white reporters had few sources in the black community, so many of the best reporters from the black press were hired for jobs in big-city newsrooms. This gave major newspapers as well as radio and TV broadcasters access to the important insiders in the civil rights movement.

Frank Bolden, who worked for the black newspaper the *Pittsburgh Courier*, found a job with the *New York Times*. Bolden said:

> The black press made me conscious of the fact that I was truly an American and I deserved everything every other American got. If it did nothing more, it made me realize that separate does not mean equal. And ever since I worked at the Courier, I have been a battler and a champion for equal rights for all American citizens, regardless of their color, race, or creed. And now gender.[9]

In 1975, 44 black journalists formed the organization that's known today as the National Association of Black Journalists. Many of its members work for the mainstream print and electronic media, but many more work for the black newspapers that continue to serve important functions in their communities. Such papers include the *Chicago Defender*, *Los Angeles Sentinel*, *Washington Afro-American*, *Philadelphia Tribune*, and *New York Amsterdam News*. About 200 black newspapers are published in about 150 different US cities as of 2020.

Black journalists may have come a long way in recent years, but it would be naive to suggest that racial bias has disappeared from the media. John Leo, a media critic for *U.S. News & World Report*, suggested the media may treat issues of racial diversity so lightly because few American newsrooms reflect the true racial composition of American society. People of color make up one-third of the population of the United States, but most professional newsrooms fall far short of reflecting that diversity. In 2018, the Pew Research Center reported that 77 percent of newsroom employees are white and 61 percent are male. These are higher percentages than US workers overall. Some people believe this is because people of color are less likely to look for a career in journalism, but studies have shown this is untrue. People of color "made up 21.4 percent of graduates with degrees in journalism or communications between 2004 and 2014, but less than half of minority graduates found full-time jobs, while two-thirds of white graduates did."[10] This trend hasn't changed over time. This lack of diversity means the stories the mainstream media

Shown here is civil rights leader Jesse Jackson reading about the news of Martin Luther King Jr.'s assassination in the *Daily Defender*. This black-owned newspaper was a major part of the civil rights movement, giving black Americans important news that the white-owned media often ignored.

Profits Drive News Coverage

During his campaign for the presidency in 2008, Democrat Barack Obama made a trip to the war zones in Afghanistan and Iraq, followed by a speech in Berlin, Germany, in front of an estimated crowd of about 200,000 people. Three major American TV networks sent their anchors to cover the speech, while dozens of other reporters followed Obama as well. A few months earlier, Republican presidential candidate John McCain also toured the war zone in Iraq. None of the networks sent their anchors, and in comparison, the McCain visit received almost no coverage in the media.

Such an obvious difference raises the question about whether Obama received favorable treatment in the media. Some people believed reporters gave Obama favorable treatment because they didn't want to be accused of racism for ignoring a black candidate.

Media critic John K. Wilson didn't think that was the case. Wilson, who writes about the media for the advocacy group Fairness & Accuracy in Reporting (FAIR), said Obama received preferential coverage because, as his speech in Berlin proved, he made more news. "Obama is on the cover of magazines because his face sells a lot more magazines than McCain's picture," Wilson wrote. "That's a pro-profit bias, not a liberal bias."[1] However, this type of for-profit coverage has been widely criticized because it shapes which stories the public is able to learn about.

1. John K. Wilson, "The Myth of Pro-Obama Media Bias," FAIR, September 15, 2008. fair.org/extra/the-myth-of-pro-obama-media-bias.

reports often don't take different points of view into account. Additionally, issues that primarily affect people of color, women, the LGBTQ+ community, and other groups are often not reported. Despite the best efforts of oppressed groups to be heard in the mainstream media, the bias they find in the press never seems to go away.

Your Opinion Matters!

1. Give some examples of bias you've seen directed at specific groups. How can you identify this kind of bias?

2. Why is it important to have watchdog groups?

3. What are some topics you think the mainstream media might ignore?

12:08

◀ Viber

🔒 politico.com   ↻

POLITICO   🔍

○ TOP NEWS

Nielsen's allies trying to rehab her image for life after Trump

Liberal activists say she was complicit in an immoral migrant child separation policy — and should be

IS NEUTRALITY POSSIBLE?

Some people believe it's impossible for the news to be unbiased. They say bias is profitable, so news outlets will keep reporting stories in ways that are obviously slanted. Many people also say the news media is one of the biggest causes of polarization in society today. Even many journalists agree on these points. In a 2018 article, AllSides—a news outlet whose stated aim is to publish stories from various perspectives to give a more balanced picture—wrote, "Everyone is biased. It's impossible to avoid. Journalists approach every story with unique life experiences that consciously and subconsciously influence the work they do ... What's more, the 24-hour news cycle operates on a business model that relies on inflaming the political divide."[1] AllSides suggested that instead of looking for one unbiased news source, people should try to get their news from a variety of reputable outlets.

Unbiased news may be an unattainable dream, but some outlets are less biased than others. One feature of a reliable news resource is that it's willing to announce corrections to its previous coverage instead of doubling down and making conflicting information sound like a problem of the opposition's

Politico is rated one of the least biased and most truthful news sources by the independent website Media Bias/Fact Check. It has been accused by the left of having an obvious right-leaning bias and vice versa, showing that sometimes when people read things they don't like, they assume bias is involved.

bias. In August 2017, *Adam Ruins Everything* aired a correction segment in which the host explained the ethics of correcting reporting mistakes and making new information known:

> We have gotten a few things wrong, but that doesn't ruin our show at all … Our research team [spends] every day calling experts, combing through sources, and fact-checking scripts to ensure that the information we present on this show is as close to the truth as possible. But they're also human, and humans sometimes make mistakes … It wouldn't be truthful to claim we were infallible [unable to be wrong]. The intellectually honest thing to do is to be transparent about our process and public about our mistakes.[2]

All journalists will report something incorrect at one point or another, either because of human error or because new information comes to light later. Admitting mistakes is one important way of correcting this type of bias.

Working to Stay Objective

Many editors and reporters at mainstream news outlets—those who are on the front lines reporting and editing the news every day—take issue with critics who suggest that they permit their personal biases to interfere with their professional responsibilities to present the news to their readers and viewers. Most will admit to harboring personal biases—that's simply part of being human—but they also insist that they don't permit their feelings about political or social issues to color their work as journalists.

One example is Shepard Smith, who was an anchor on Fox News until October 2019. Although Smith worked at the conservative news channel and has conservative views, he generally seemed to make an effort to report the news as truthfully as possible, even when it went against his own views or the network's. For example, after Hurricane Maria hit Puerto Rico in 2017, Smith debunked a false news story reported by his own network that said supplies weren't being distributed to Puerto Rican victims because truckers in Puerto Rico were on strike and refusing to deliver the items. This rumor originated with President Donald Trump, who blamed the truckers for not doing enough after San Juan's mayor Carmen Yulin Cruz criticized the president's administration for its slow response. According to Smith:

> *Of course, the president mentioned the truckers ... The biggest problem on the island is the distribution of supplies, we're told ... Some of the truckers can't be reached because there's no communication working in so many areas still.*
>
> *Reports that a union truckers' strike added to the problems are not true ... They are, in fact, fake news, spread largely, it appears, by a website called Conservative Treehouse and then over Twitter and Facebook. Again, there is no trucker's strike. That's fake news. The truckers in Puerto Rico are victims too.*[3]

When Smith announced his departure from Fox News, many people were stunned, as he'd been with the network since 1996. Some speculated that he quit because he felt pressured to compromise his journalistic ethics. In an article for *Forbes* magazine, Terina Allen wrote, "As Shepard Smith signed off from his last show, he proclaimed that 'facts will win the day.' We can reasonably surmise that Smith felt some sort of pressure to compromise his integrity going forward in order to remain in the good graces of network executives."[4]

Sometimes the knowledge that bias exists in the media can lead people to see bias where there is none. For example, early in 2008, NBC correspondent Lee Cowan admitted on the air that as he covered then-presidential candidate Barack Obama, he found himself overwhelmed by the thousands of people who were flocking to Obama's speeches. "From a reporter's point of view," Cowan admitted, "it's almost hard to remain objective. It's infectious, the energy, I think."[5] Critics immediately attacked Cowan and NBC for showing a bias toward Obama, but NBC anchor Brian Williams was quick to defend the network's objectivity. He said:

> *Lee was talking about the swirl of excitement that has hit the Obama campaign ... the crowds, the hoopla—all of it. Today we*

Shepard Smith was one cable news anchor who was consistently
committed to reporting the facts of a story with as little bias as possible.

learned that rival political efforts were spinning this as some kind of "bias" on the part of either Lee, or me, or this News Division, and that's just ridiculous. My response is as it always is in these situations: look at it again, listen to what's being said, and judge us by the quality and fairness of our journalism.[6]

Keeping the Media Accountable

News organizations are not always insensitive to charges of bias. For example, many online newspapers have started publishing the contact information of their reporters so readers can contact them directly to discuss issues of bias in their stories. Most also invite readers to add their own comments underneath the stories, which makes it easier for people to see others' support or objections.

Dave Winer, who runs the blog *Scripting News*, said his readers are constantly challenging his facts, which he feels has made him pay close attention to accuracy and fairness. He also said many bloggers have taken steps to help ensure fairness and guarantee accuracy to readers. According to Winer, many bloggers now include links to the source materials on which they base their commentaries. These sources often include news stories published on newspapers' websites, reports issued by government agencies, speeches by political leaders, and transcripts of testimony of witnesses who testify before congressional committees. Therefore, if a blogger takes issue with comments made by a politician, blog readers can instantly read what the politician had to say in their own words and judge for themselves. By making such sources available, Winer said, blog readers can immediately verify the accuracy and fairness of the bloggers' commentaries.

Many groups are making it their business to similarly judge the media for their accuracy and fairness. Some of these organizations have been funded by foundations and other nonpartisan, or nonpolitical, organizations to maintain a true public dialogue on press bias and similar issues that surround the news media. The intentions of other groups are not as clear. On the surface, these groups claim to monitor the media, but in some cases, they have hidden agendas: They have been established by liberal or conservative groups for the purpose of enhancing their arguments about bias.

One website, Media Bias/Fact Check, is a comprehensive list of news outlets grouped by bias. The categories of bias include left, left-center, least biased, right-center, right, pro-science, conspiracy/pseudoscience, questionable sources, and satire. Each entry includes where the news source falls on this spectrum, how trustworthy its facts are, and a short synopsis of the content and reliability of the source. For instance, in the case of the left-leaning feminist blog *Feministing*, Media Bias/Fact Check wrote:

> *In review, Feministing has a strong left wing bias in reporting as most articles favor the political left and criticize conservative policies. There is strong use of loaded words in headlines such as this: WHY JOE ARPAIO DESERVES TO BURN IN HELL (A LAUNDRY LIST). Interestingly, this same article is impeccably sourced to credible media sources and is 100% evidence based. So, while the headline may be sensational the content of the article is factual.*[7]

Media Bias/Fact Check consistently evaluates news outlets and updates their rankings as needed. For example, while it classified *Feministing* as highly factual in 2017, it later downgraded the website's factual accuracy to "mixed" after one of its articles was proven seriously wrong by Politifact, another fact-checking website.

Another website dedicated to stopping the spread of false information is Snopes. This website, which was founded in 1994 by David Mikkelson, employs dedicated fact-checkers who verify internet rumors, viral social media posts, and questionable news reports. The articles that can be found on the website range from current events to urban legends, and Snopes is considered by many to be one of the most reputable and least biased sources of information currently available. In late 2019, Snopes investigated a fake news website called The BL and reported it multiple times to Facebook. After being ignored by the social media giant for several months, Snopes openly challenged Facebook to explain why it wasn't removing The BL's posts, "suggesting that Facebook's response to The BL was 'inconsistent with their own public statements that proclaim a commitment to rooting out such abuse.'"[8] One week after this challenge, Facebook announced that it had removed The BL's pages, but the company's statement claimed that its employees had done the investigative work themselves.

The website Snopes is committed to exposing fake news, urban legends, and inaccurate reporting.

When news outlets recirculate biased and untrue information, people may read the same rumor dozens of times, making them think it's true. Using websites such as Snopes and Media Bias/Fact Check can help people avoid being tricked this way.

Unfortunately, assessments produced by other so-called media watchdog groups may not be as neutral as the groups would like readers to believe. Many self-described media watchdog groups whose names would suggest impartiality actually have hidden purposes. For example, Accuracy in Media (AIM) and the Media Research Center (MRC) are both sponsored by conservative activists and are dedicated to exposing what they believe to be cases of liberal reporting bias. On the other side, the group Fairness & Accuracy in Reporting (FAIR) claims to be unbiased, but critics have complained that it more often finds fault with the conservative press than with the liberal press. This doesn't mean that everything they say is untrue, but it does mean people should be skeptical of what they read on these websites.

Stay Skeptical

The credibility of the press and news media has seen a steady decline in recent years, and the question of believability and accuracy is regularly debated. Surveys have shown how much the public trust in reporting has declined. In 2012, the Pew Research Center reported that the favorable rating of the mainstream media—excluding local news sources—was 56 percent and the negative view was 44 percent. In 2019, Gallup reported that only 41 percent of Americans felt the mass media was trustworthy.

Striking a balance between trusting and distrusting the press is becoming increasingly important. Media literacy helps people do this, although it's still possible for people to be fooled on occasion. News outlets do frequently report important information, even when it's slanted in one direction or another. Ignoring that information completely is foolish, especially since biased doesn't necessarily mean false. A headline may be biased and attention-grabbing and the language used in the article may make the author's opinions clear, but it's

Is Bias Ever Acceptable?

Seth Ackerman, a contributor to *Extra!*, a magazine published by FAIR, believes bias in the media may not be such a bad thing. After all, he pointed out, British newspapers such as the *Times* of London, which is conservative, and the *Guardian*, which is liberal, have long been known for their biases. However, he has said, each newspaper is successful and enjoys a wide and dedicated readership.

The difference may be that these newspapers make no secret of their biases—unlike American media outlets that often claim to be objective and yet are clearly biased. For example, Ackerman said, when Fox News first went on the air in 1996, it adopted the slogan "Fair and Balanced," a motto that Ackerman and others found curious, given Fox's clearly conservative leanings. Ackerman said:

> *Some have suggested that Fox's conservative point of view and its Republican leanings render the network inherently unworthy as a news outlet. FAIR believes that view is misguided. The United States is unusual, perhaps even unique, in having a journalistic culture so fiercely wedded to the elusive notion of "objective" news ... In Great Britain, papers like the conservative Times of London and the left-leaning Guardian deliver consistently excellent coverage while making no secret of their respective points of view. There's nothing keeping American journalists from doing the same.*[1]

1. Seth Ackerman, "The Most Biased Name in News," FAIR, July 1, 2001, fair.org/extra/the-most-biased-name-in-news.

possible to write a factually correct yet biased article. However, blindly accepting everything the media says—especially when it comes from only one source—is also unwise. Furthermore, trusting viral social media posts, memes, and websites without clear factual sources instead of news sources that have established their trustworthiness over many years has proven to be dangerous. Dismissing something as "fake news" when it doesn't align with the beliefs a person already holds undermines democracy and makes it easy for untrustworthy people and organizations to take advantage of citizens. Media literacy is a skill that's becoming increasingly crucial in today's society.

Your Opinion Matters!

1. What do you think are the most important media literacy skills you can develop?
2. What can you do to fight bias and fake news?
3. Do you trust the news? Why or why not?

The following are some suggestions for taking what you've just read and applying that information to your everyday life.

- Do some basic fact-checking before you share anything you find online.

- Learn more about media literacy and practice it daily.

- Don't knowingly share false or misleading things even if they align with your views.

- Debunk fake, misleading, or heavily biased news when you see it.

- If you see that someone has mistaken satire for the truth, politely let them know.

- Don't yell at someone who's shared something that turned out to be false; everyone gets fooled sometimes.

- Think about your own biases so you can examine how they affect the way you consume news media.

NOTES

Introduction: Becoming Media Savvy

1. Linda A. Klein, "A Free Press Is Necessary for a Strong Democracy," *ABA Journal*, May 1, 2017, www.abajournal.com/magazine/article/free_press_linda_klein.

Chapter One: Understanding Bias and Fake News

1. "Ethical Journalism," *New York Times*, accessed January 28, 2020, www.nytimes.com/editorial-standards/ethical-journalism.html.

2. Quoted in Jack Shafer, "Annenberg's Ticket Out of Hell," Slate, May 22, 2006, www.slate.com/id/2142154.

3. Quoted in Melody Kramer, "Is Media Bias Really Rampant? Ask the Man Who Studies It for a Living," *Poynter*, October 24, 2016, www.poynter.org/news/media-bias-really-rampant-ask-man-who-studies-it-living.

4. Quoted in Paul Rosenberg, "Not Fake News: Major Study Finds No 'Liberal Bias' in Media—but There Are Other Problems," Salon, January 5, 2020, www.salon.com/2020/01/05/not-fake-news-major-study-finds-no-liberal-bias-in-media-but-there-are-other-problems.

5. Kara Hackett, "A Reporter's Take on 'Liberal Media Bias,'" *HuffPost*, modified October 5, 2017, www.huffingtonpost.com/entry/a-reporters-take-on-liberal-media-bias_us_591a5277e4b086d2d0d8d22b.

Chapter Two: Combining News and Entertainment

1. Quoted in "Content Analysis of O'Reilly's Rhetoric Finds Spin to Be a 'Factor,'" Indiana University, modified May 2, 2007, newsinfo.iu.edu/news-archive/5535.html.

2. Brian Stelter, "Gotcha TV: Crews Stalk Bill O'Reilly's Targets," *New York Times*, April 15, 2009, www.nytimes.com/2009/04/16/arts/television/16ambush.html.

3. Quoted in John Timpane, "Fox News Finds the Right Stuff in the Age of Obama," *Pittsburgh Post-Gazette*, May 13, 2009, www.post-gazette.com/ae/tv-radio/2009/05/13/Fox-News-finds-right-stuff-in-the-age-of-Obama/stories/200905130177.

4. William Poundstone, "A Rigorous Scientific Look into the 'Fox News Effect,'" *Forbes*, July 21, 2016, www.forbes.com/sites/quora/2016/07/21/a-rigorous-scientific-look-into-the-fox-news-effect.

5. LastWeekTonight, "Alex Jones: Last Week Tonight with John Oliver (HBO)," YouTube video, 22:21, July 30, 2017, www.youtube.com/watch?v=WyGq6rjcc3Q.

6. LastWeekTonight, "Alex Jones," YouTube video.

7. Josh Owens, "I Worked for Alex Jones. I Regret It," *New York Times*, December 5, 2019, www.nytimes.com/2019/12/05/magazine/alex-jones-infowars.html.

8. Quoted in Josh Constine, "Facebook Puts Link to 10 Tips for Spotting 'False News' Atop Feed," *TechCrunch*, April 6, 2017, techcrunch.com/2017/04/06/facebook-puts-link-to-10-tips-for-spotting-false-news-atop-feed.

Chapter Three: News on the Internet

1. Quoted in "The Rise and Rise of Fake News," BBC, November 6, 2016. www.bbc.com/news/blogs-trending-37846860.

2. "The Rise and Rise of Fake News," BBC.

3. Emma Woollacott, "The Viral Spread of Ebola Rumors," *Forbes*, October 9, 2014, www.forbes.com/sites/emmawoollacott/2014/10/09/the-viral-spread-of-ebola-rumors.

4. Quoted in Mary-Rose Papandrea, "Citizen Journalism and the Reporter's Privilege," *Minnesota Law Review* 91, no. 3 (2006): p. 528.

5. Sue Shellenbarger, "Most Students Don't Know When News Is Fake, Stanford Study Finds," *Wall Street Journal*, modified November 21, 2016, www.wsj.com/articles/most-students-dont-know-when-news-is-fake-stanford-study-finds-1479752576.

6. LastWeekTonight, "Native Advertising: Last Week Tonight with John Oliver (HBO)," YouTube video, 11:22, August 3, 2014, www.youtube.com/watch?v=E_F5GxCwizc.

7. Suzanne Ciechalski and Rima Abdelkader, "Misinformation Swirls Online After Iran's Missile Attack on U.S. Targets in Iraq," NBC News, January 9, 2020, www.nbcnews.com/news/world/misinformation-swirls-online-after-iran-s-missile-attack-u-s-n1112771.

8. Quoted in Ciechalski and Abdelkader, "Misinformation Swirls Online."

9. Craig Timberg, "Russian Propaganda Effort Helped Spread 'Fake News' During Election, Experts Say," *Washington Post*, November 24, 2016, www.washingtonpost.com/business/economy/russian-propaganda-effort-helped-spread-fake-news-during-election-experts-say/2016/11/24/793903b6-8a40-4ca9-b712-716af66098fe_story.html.

10. Abigail Abrams, "Here's What We Know so Far About Russia's 2016 Meddling," *TIME*, April 18, 2019, time.com/5565991/russia-influence-2016-election.

Chapter Four: Targets of Bias

1. Jessica Wakeman, "Misogyny's Greatest Hits," FAIR, June 1, 2008, fair.org/extra/misogynys-greatest-hits.

2. Mary Bowerman, "Fox News' Brit Hume Under Fire for Saying Clinton 'Not Necessarily Attractive,'" *USA Today*, September 28, 2016, www.usatoday.com/story/news/politics/onpolitics/2016/09/27/fox-news-presidential-debate-hillary-clinton-appearance-brit-hume/91155602.

3. Adrienne LaFrance, "I Analyzed a Year of My Reporting for Gender Bias (Again)," *The Atlantic*, February 17, 2016, www.theatlantic.com/technology/archive/2016/02/gender-diversity-journalism/463023.

4. LaFrance, "I Analyzed a Year of My Reporting."

5. "A Note to Our Readers," *Esquire*, April 17, 2009, www.esquire.com/news-politics/a5706/note-to-our-readers-041309.

6. Quoted in Leigh Ann Carey, "What the Media Get Wrong in Coverage of LGBTQ Politicians," *Columbia Journalism Review*, July 31, 2019, www.cjr.org/criticism/lgbtq-politicians-media.php.

7. Carey, "What the Media Get Wrong."

8. Gabriel Arana, "Islamophobic Media Coverage Is Out of Control. It Needs to Stop," *HuffPost*, modified November 19, 2015, www.huffpost.com/entry/islamophobia-mainstream-media-paris-terrorist-attacks_n_564cb277e4b08c74b7339984.

9. "Interview Transcripts: Frank Bolden," PBS, 1998. www.pbs.org/black-press/film/transcripts/bolden.html.

10. Gillian B. White, "Where Are All the Minority Journalists?," *The Atlantic*, July 24, 2015, www.theatlantic.com/business/archive/2015/07/minorities-in-journalism/399461.

Chapter Five: Is Neutrality Possible?

1. Billy Binion, "Does Unbiased News Really Exist?," AllSides, April 10, 2018, www.allsides.com/blog/does unbiased-news-really-exist.

2. CollegeHumor, "Adam Ruins Everything Corrects ITSELF!," YouTube video, 6:13, August 30, 2017, www.youtube.com/watch?v=-ijI_kGG1eg.

3. Quoted in Taylor Link, "Shepard Smith Debunks 'Fake News' That Puerto Rico Truck Drivers Are on Strike," Salon, October 4, 2017, www.salon.com/2017/10/04/shepard-smith-debunks-fake-news-that-puerto-rican-truck-drivers-are-on-strike.

4. Terina Allen, "This Is Why Shepard Smith Ended His Career With Fox News," *Forbes*, October 12, 2019, www.forbes.com/sites/terinaallen/2019/10/12/this-is-why-shepard-smith-ended-his-career-with-fox-news.

5. Quoted in "Journalists Admitting Liberal Bias, Part One," Media Research Center, accessed January 30, 2020, www.mrc.org/media-bias-101/journalists-admitting-liberal-bias-part-one.

6. Quoted in Tim Graham, "Williams Denies Pro-Barack Bias at NBC: 'That's Just Ridiculous,'" MRC NewsBusters, January 9, 2008, www.newsbusters.org/blogs/nb/tim-graham/2008/01/09/williams-denies-pro-barack-bias-nbc-thats-just-ridiculous.

7. "Feministing," Media Bias/Fact Check, accessed January 30, 2020, mediabiasfactcheck.com/feministing.

8. Alex Kasprak and Jordan Liles, "Facebook Removes Deceptive BL Network Following Snopes' Reporting," Snopes, December 20, 2019, www.snopes.com/news/2019/12/20/facebook-removes-the-bl-pages.

FOR MORE INFORMATION

Books: Nonfiction

Duhig, Holly. *Media and the News*. New York, NY: Crabtree Publishing, 2019.

Fromowitz, Lori. *12 Great Moments That Changed Newspaper History*. North Mankato, MN: 12-Story Library, 2015.

Mooney, Carla. *Asking Questions About How the News Is Created*. Ann Arbor, MI: Cherry Lake Publishing, 2016.

Steele, Philip. *Race and Crime*. New York, NY: Crabtree Publishing, 2017.

Books: Fiction

Clements, Andrew. *The Landry News*. New York, NY: Atheneum Books for Young Readers, 2000.

Myers, Walter Dean, and Peter Francis James. *Darnell Rock Reporting*. New York, NY: Yearling, 1994.

Websites

Accuracy in Media (AIM)

www.aim.org

AIM makes it clear that it searches for liberal bias in the media. Visitors to the group's website can find many examples of reporting that AIM feels are biased against conservatives.

Black Press USA

www.blackpressusa.com

This group showcases the work of black journalists and is dedicated to telling the stories of the black community in the United States. It also features commentaries from world-renowned black scholars, journalists, and activists.

Factitious

factitious.augamestudio.com

This game lets users test how skilled they are at spotting fake news.

Fairness & Accuracy in Reporting (FAIR)

www.fair.org

FAIR is dedicated to reporting on media bias and maintains a website that includes many resources about unbalanced reporting.

Media Bias/Fact Check

mediabiasfactcheck.com

This website allows internet users to check how biased and how factual various news outlets are.

Organizations

News Leaders Association (NLA)
209 Reynolds Journalism Institute
Missouri School of Journalism
Columbia, MO 65211
www.newsleaders.org
twitter.com/NewsEditors
Formerly known as the American Society of News Editors and the Associated Press Media Editors, NLA sets ethical standards for newspaper journalists, including rules regarding bias in their reporting. The organization defends freedom of the press and unbiased reporting.

Center for Media and Public Affairs (CMPA)
2338 South Queen Street
Arlington, VA 22202
www.cmpa.com
twitter.com/cmpaatgmu
CMPA is a nonprofit organization that performs scientific studies of the media's impact on American society. Many of those studies have examined bias.

Federal Communications Commission (FCC)
445 12th Street SW
Washington, DC 20554
www.fcc.gov
www.instagram.com/fcc
twitter.com/fcc
www.youtube.com/fcc
The FCC regulates broadcasters in the United States. This government organization's website includes many articles and other resources on the history and laws governing access to the airwaves.

Pew Research Center: Journalism and Media
1615 L Street NW, Suite 800
Washington, DC 20036
www.journalism.org
twitter.com/pewresearch
www.youtube.com/user/PewResearchCenter
The Pew Research Center conducts studies on many topics,
including journalism and the media.

Snopes
www.snopes.com
twitter.com/snopes
This website conducts research to determine whether rumors
circulated on the internet are true or false. Users can submit stories
they think should be fact-checked to the Contact Us page.

INDEX

ABOUT THE AUTHOR

Jennifer Lombardo earned her BA in English from the University at Buffalo and still resides in Buffalo, New York, with her cat, Chip. She has helped write a number of books for young adults on topics ranging from world history to body image. In her spare time, she enjoys cross-stitching, hiking, and volunteering with Habitat for Humanity.